MASTERING THE IPHONE 11 PRO AND PRO MAX CAMERA

SMART PHONE PHOTOGRAPHY TAKING PICTURES LIKE A PRO EVEN AS A BEGINNER

JAMES NINO

© 2019 James Nino

All rights reserved.

You are welcome to join the Fan's Corner, here

Mastering the iPhone 11 Pro and Pro Max Camera

SmartPhone Photography Taking Pictures like a Pro
Even as a Beginner

James Nino

Disclaimer

i

Introduction

Hey, congratulation on purchasing Mastering the iPhone 11 Pro and Pro Max Camera book. This book is a must-have book for anyone who wants to use his or her iPhone 11 Pro to start taking stunning photos.

This book will open your eyes to many of the basic functions that the iPhone 11 Pro and Pro Max camera can be used for as well as some advanced functions that may not be too obvious to users of the iPhone 11 Pro. For those who already have older versions of the iPhone and have difficulty locating some of their favorite icons, this book will show you where they have been moved to and the most effective ways of using them to take amazing pictures.

Quite often, the manuals shipped with our devices tend not to do enough justice to the subject of the device at other times, they can be overwhelming. Many other "Get Started Guides" are sometimes too thin and do not really solve any problem, which is why this book is a real gem.

This book will get you acquainted with the mobile phone you carry around you that you can also use for your photography device whenever you go on a trip, attend an event, visit a location, or casting a scene. Knowing how to get more from the digital camera in your pocket is what this book is about, after all, after spending so much to get your iPhone 11 Pro, you naturally would want to get more out of it.

This book will help you know how to use the camera on your iPhone 11 Pro better and help you optimize the camera features in a lot more ways than you have ever imagined.

As you open the pages of this book, you will be exposed to a wide range of fantastic photos and video tools that you had probably overlooked as ordinary symbols to a position where you now know how to use them.

For those who order this book while on vacation, this book can help you improve on your use of your iPhone camera, especially for those things you did not know it could do. You will find that this book is quite worth the time and money spent on it and highly recommended to anyone who uses their iPhone 11 Pro and Pro Max to take pictures. You can start using your iPhone 11 Pro camera and start taking the kind of photos that nobody will even believe were shot by you with an iPhone.

Contents to Expect

Chapter 1

❧❧❧❧❧❧

Introducing the iPhone 11 Pro

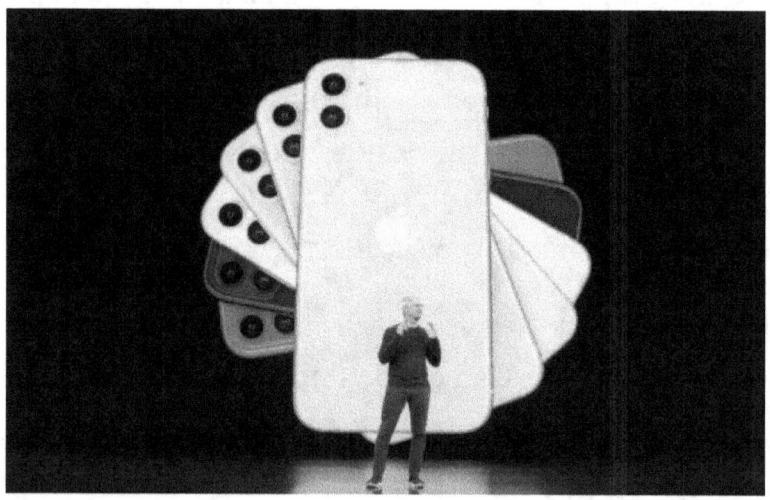

The announcement of the release of iPhone 11, iPhone 11 Pro and the iPhone 11 Pro Max by Apple in September 2019 saw the introduction of a new set of gadgets for their teeming customers. Apple claims on their release that the iPhone 11 Pro contains what it says is the most significant camera upgrade ever to feature on an iPhone, and it is not hard to see why once you handle the iPhone Pro. Simply put, the exceptional camera has been significantly redesigned and is the biggest upgrade to the iPhone 11 Pro compared to the previous versions of the iPhone family.

Using the iPhone 11 Pro to take pictures is as easy as it's always been in previous versions of the iPhones only that now you can make it do more than those versions if you only knew how to find your way around the interface. Compared to what you may be used to in earlier versions of the iPhone, some controls and settings in the iPhone 11 Pro no longer exist while many others have been moved to new locations, including some changes in the layout of the phone's camera app. The camera app on the iPhone 11 Pro is at first glance similar to the old iPhone Camera app only that the new app has a great deal of depth, which makes it able to take crisp photos with minimal effort even when the lighting is limited.

One of the first visual observation you will notice on the app are the new set of controls at the top of the screen, the image data from the ultra-wide camera which blends with the transparent toolbar area around the main viewfinder, the flip camera icon which now has a new design, an additional zoom control, and a triangle disclosure indicator. Apple moved the toggle settings for features like the timer and filters because they felt those features weren't among the most frequently used functions on their iPhone models.

Software and interface changes are not the only things that differentiate the iPhone 11 Pro from other iPhone versions. The cameras on the iPhone were already very good at taking great daytime pictures, but the new iPhone 11 Pro takes their photography to a whole new level. This is mostly because the iPhone 11 Pro has a triple-lens setup at the back, which enables the phone to expand its capabilities.

To take advantage of these hardware features is an expanded software capability that enables it to produce crystal clear pictures, among other new functions like the Night mode and the Quick Take video. There is also a unique feature that allows users to zoom out on an image even though you had previously captured it with some parts that seem to be missing.

These hardware and software make the iPhone 11 Pro to be touted to be one of the best iPhones ever to be produced by Apple when you consider the ingenuity in combining technology with the phone's high-level photography. The majority of the iPhone's 11 Pro functions involve knowing what and how to tap, which is what helps to ensure that the photos shot with the iPhone 11 Pro even if taken by a novice come out crisp, amazing and sharp. This phone runs on iOS 13 with a high-level dual-sensor for the rear cameras and also powered by Apple's new A13 Bionic chip.

The four available colors for the iPhone 11 Pro for buyers to choose from include Gold, Midnight Green, Silver, and Space Grey.

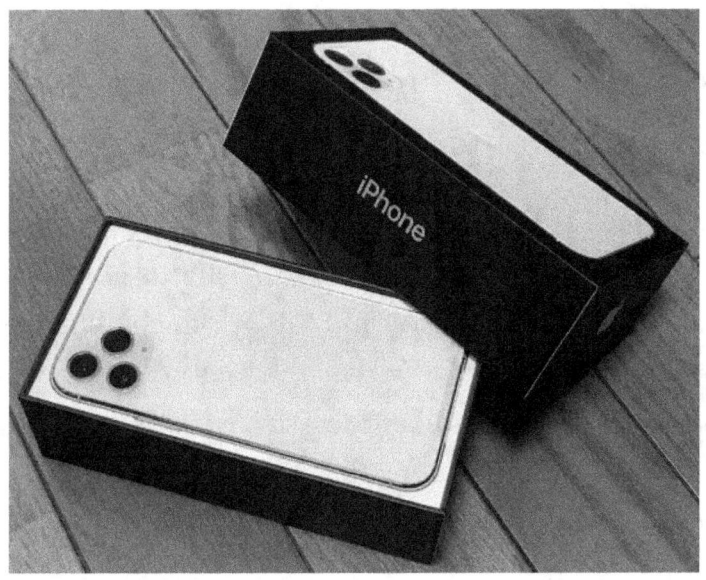

Figure 1: Unveiling the iPhone 11 Pro

According to Apple, the iPhone 11 Pro is made from the toughest glass ever to grace the glass body of a smartphone and offers an amazing resistance to dust and water with its IP rating of IP68, which helps to improve its reliability and durability.

It's rated to be able to stay up to a depth of water of up to 2M or 6.5 feet for a period of up to 30 minutes. Although an IP68 rating can withstand immersion in water, it is advisable to limit the phone's exposure to water to just splashes, accidental exposure to liquid, and maybe rain.

For sounds, it equally supports Dolby Atmos and Spatial audio, which enables it to offer a truly impressive sound experience.

The iPhone 11 Pro's Technical Specs

The iPhone 11 Pro is a 5.80-inch touchscreen Apple phone that comes shipped with iOS 13 and is powered by a Hexa-core Apple A13 Bionic CPU, which retains the 7nm architecture as in previous versions. As at the time of writing this book, this processor is acclaimed to be Apple's fastest chip on the market in terms of performance and support for the graphical demands of the iPhone 11 Pro.

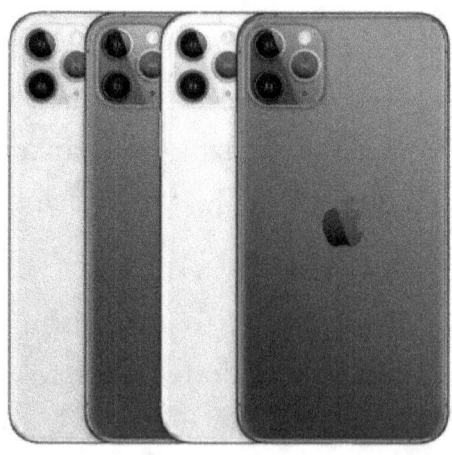

Figure 2: Various Colors for Shipping iPhone 11

The iPhone 11 Pro features dual GSM SIMs for Nano-SIM and eSIM cards.

The Intel modem chip that comes with iPhone 11 Pro supports Gigabit-class LTE, 802.11 a/b/g/n/ac Wi-Fi 6 support, 3G, 4G, and Band 40 support, Bluetooth 5.0, UI ultra-wideband chip for better spatial awareness with better indoor tracking capabilities. It also has sensors that it uses for its gyroscope, ambient light sensor, accelerometer, compass/ magnetometer, barometer, and proximity sensor. Not to be left out is its support for face unlocks with 3D face recognition.

The iPhone 11 Pro has support for wireless charging, including proprietary fast charging.

The battery life of the iPhone 11 Pro is terrific and is powered by a non-removable 3046mAh battery.

The iPhone 11's Pro Design and Display

The iPhone 11 Pro shares similar physical attributes as its predecessor iPhone XR but has a noticeable camera bump on its back that houses the new triple camera array, which the XR does not have. Such camera bumps are not entirely new in the mobile phone industry, as a matter of fact, many iPhone enthusiasts have been demanding that the iPhone improves the quality of its camera, especially when compared to other Android phones. However, unlike the camera bump of Samsung Galaxy S10, Huawei P30 Pro, and other Chinese manufacturing competitors, that of the iPhone 11 Pro is considerably chunkier.

Apple also opted to retain the divisive screen notch from the days of the iPhone X even though many other Android competitors have since abandoned that technology for more subtle solutions like the teardrop notch, pop-up, and cut out camera.

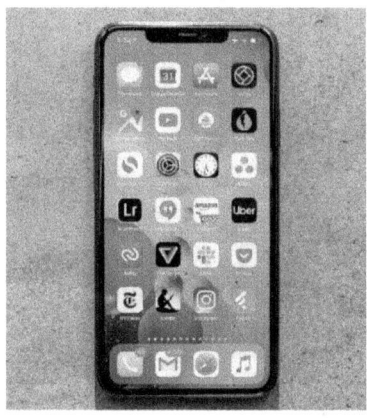

Figure 3: iPhone Screen Display with Resolution

The phone comes with a resolution of 1125 x 2436 pixels and a pixel density of 458 pixels per inch (PPI) with a contrast ratio of 1M:1 for its LCD. Against the expectation of many, Apple has opted to go with the "Super Retina XDR" for its all-screen OLED Multi-Touch display. The display equally has support for Apple's newest advancement in technology that allows for tapping to wake up or activate the screen, Haptic Touch, swipe gesture in place of the Touch ID Home button, wide color range that enables it to provide a realistic color and a True Tone, useful in matching the ambient light to the display's white balance.

iPhone 11 Pro Camera

If there is one feature that was consistently highlighted as a significant advantage over previous editions of the iPhone, it has to be the iPhone 11 Pro's camera or cameras. The iPhone 11 Pro comes with three rear cameras that include the standard wide-angle camera, an ultra-wide-angle camera with a 120-degree field of view, and a telephoto camera lens. Switching between these cameras is, however, remarkably easy and can be executed by flips of on-screen buttons.

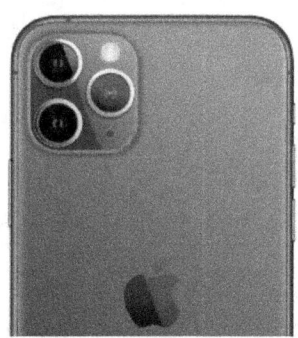

Figure 4: Triple iPhone Camera Array

The ultra-wide-angle camera can capture up to four times more scenes compared to what the standard wide-angle

8

lens can capture from the same distance from the subject, which makes it a good way of capturing architecture images, landscape photos, tight shots, group pictures, and many other creative pictures.

The iPhone 11 Pro's camera interface has also undergone some changes that allow users to have that great user experience when trying to capture scenes outside the frame through the use of the ultra-wide-angle camera. It also supports 2x optical zoom out as well as a digital zoom of up to 5x.

The addition by Apple of a new Night Mode that takes advantage of the iPhone's high processing capabilities combined with the new wide camera sensor to create crisp, bright, clear photos even in conditions that have very low lighting.

The iPhone 11 Pro also comes with next-generation Smart HDR, which allows for better recognition of people by differentiating them from the rest of the shot. Even though this feature preserves the background elements, it tends to ensure that faces retain their natural-looking skin tones, highlights, shadows, and gestures. The Next-generation Smart HDR uses machine learning in the capturing of natural-looking images that help improve the highlight and shadow detail.

Chapter 2

ೞೲೞೲೞೲ

About the Apple iPhone 11 Pro Camera

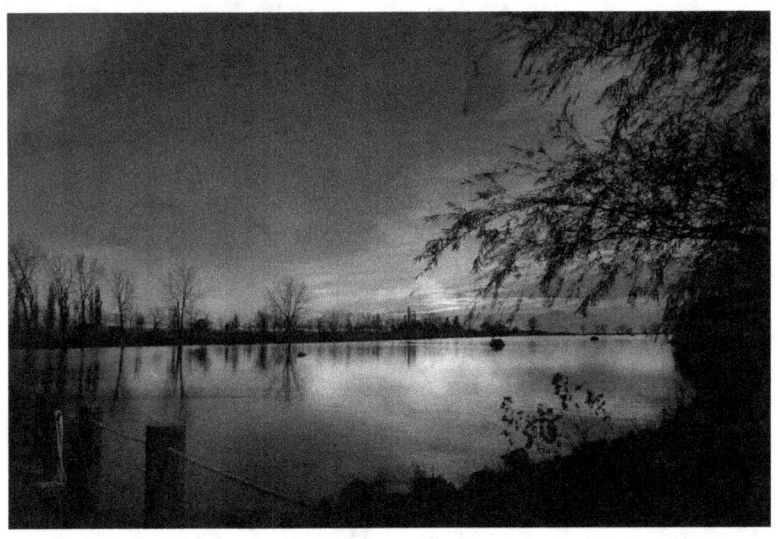

The iPhone 11 Pro has one front camera and three rear cameras. The front camera uses a TrueDepth Camera System, which aids its Face ID recognition feature in the improvement of the phone's security. Face ID is now faster by up to 30% and works from a much farther distance, wider angle range, and still very secure. That means that the phone is now able to recognize you even from a considerable distance from the phone and can open itself when you are walking towards it.

The front-facing 12-megapixel camera of the iPhone 11 Pro is an upgrade to the 7-megapixel camera that came with the iPhone XR, which makes it suitable to be used for both selfies and slofies.

The iPhone 11 Pro's new front-facing camera makes it easy to switch from portrait mode into landscape mode and vice versa, which allows for the capturing of more objects within a frame. It is equally able to capture 120 fps slo-mo videos, which is what enables a new feature call Slofies.

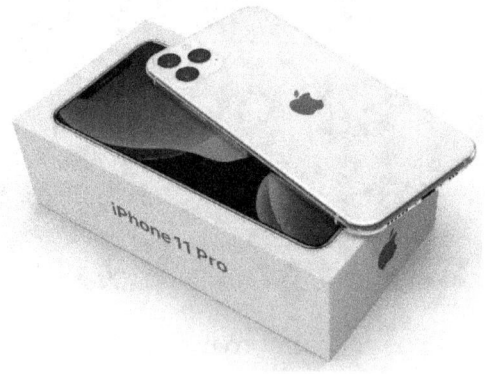

Figure 5: iPhone 11 Pro with Amazing Capability

These slow-motion videos are similar to the slo-mo videos associated with the rear-facing camera in previous iPhones. The new camera is, however, capable of recording up to 60 fps videos when in 4k mode and provides support for extended dynamic range videos at 30 fps.

Slofie is not the only feature the iPhone 11 Pro's TrueDepth Camera System supports, it also has support for animated 3D emoji characters called Animoji and Memoji, which are frequently used to simulate the way we want a person's face to appear. Where Animoji provides animal styled emojis, the Memoji offers customizable avatars that the user can personalize.

The iPhone 11 Pro model is the first Apple phone to have an upgraded triple-lens rear camera system that includes a primary camera with an f/1.8 6-element 12-megapixel wide-angle lens with a focal length of 26mm which is equivalent to a 13mm DSLR lens, a second camera with an f/2.4 5-element 12-megapixel ultra-wide-angle lens and a focal length of 13mm and a third camera with an f/2.0 aperture 12-megapixel teleport lens. The telephoto lens has support for 2x optical zoom out even though it does not have the optical zoom feature. The iPhone 11 Pro also has support for a front-facing f/2.2 aperture 12-megapixel camera for selfies and pictures from the front.

The iPhone 11 Pro model also uses its standard wide-angle camera to support Optical Image Stabilization. The combination of the standard wide-angle lens, teleport photos, and the ultra-wide-angle lens is what gives the iPhone 11 Pro its powerful camera capabilities.

The triple-lens system on the iPhone 11 Pro models makes it more suitable for capturing portrait images of many people by using its Wide and Telephoto framing in Portrait Mode.

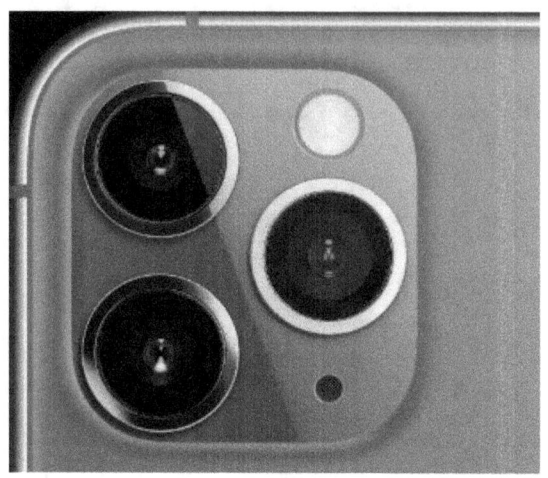

Figure 6: The Three Camera Types of iPhone 11 Pro

Apple iPhone 11 Pro Camera Features

One outstanding feature of the iPhone 11 camera is its ability to capture a space that is up to four times more than a standard camera view can capture by using its ultra-wide feature.

Another outstanding feature the iPhone 11 Pro has over its predecessors is its ability to capture pictures even in the dark, using an intelligent machine learning, computational algorithm that makes the phone take multiple shots in night mode and then fuse them to create a crisp, clear and visible image from objects that even the naked eye cannot see because of how dark the environment is. So, when next you are in a dark room, and you suspect there is someone or something else there, you can just take a shot in the direction you suspect the object is located and take a picture.

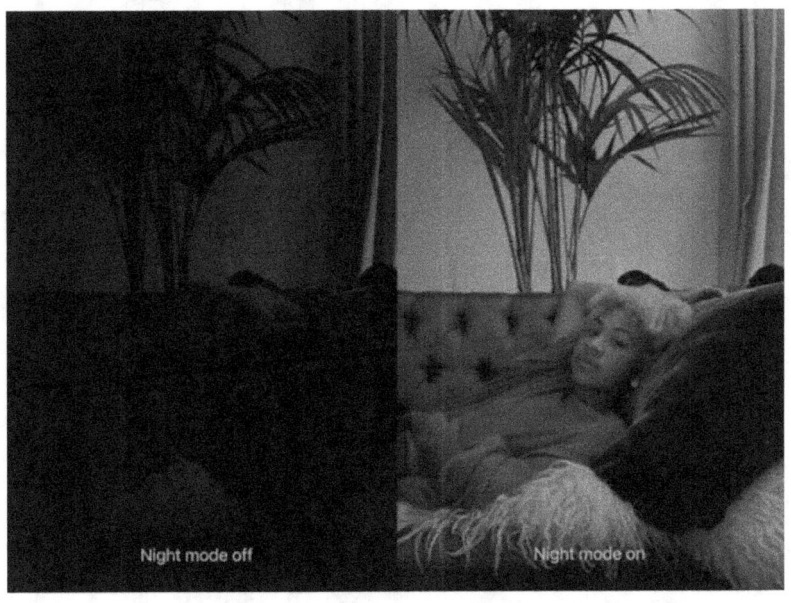

Figure 7: Comparing Night Mode On and Night Mode Off

Nonetheless, photos are not the only area where the iPhone 11 Pro excels, there is equally a new QuickTake feature that enables users to take rapid video clips without having to switch to video mode when taking still pictures by tapping and holding the shutter button quickly.

14

Lovers of social media will definitely love the slow-motion selfie videos which Apple has decided to call slofies. This feature uses the TrueDepth camera capability of the 12-megapixel sensor front camera, which also has support for 4k video capture.

Relevant Camera Settings to Know

The iPhone 11 Pro has a very powerful camera that requires a user knowing how to effectively take advantage of it by learning how to tweak the iPhone camera settings. Many of these settings are not peculiar to the iPhone cameras alone, they are also useful in the photography world and among photo enthusiasts.

Focus

This is a very dominant feature in any camera for someone that wants to take pictures that are crystal clear, not less when the person is using an iPhone 11 Pro.

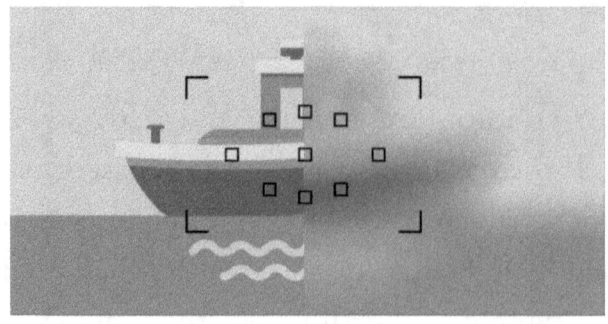

Figure 8: Camera Focus for Digital Camera

Failure to consider focus can lead to blurry images that can affect the reputation of the iPhone camera.

Those who are not camera professionals are, however, able to get by because of the tremendous depth of field that the iPhone 11 Pro has, which makes it able to ensure that both the background and the foreground are sharp with its automatic feature.

Exposure

Another critical feature that photographers play around with when utilizing cameras is exposure. Although many digital cameras can adjust their camera's exposure automatically, many other users prefer to be able to control that themselves, especially when the camera is not able to get it on its own.

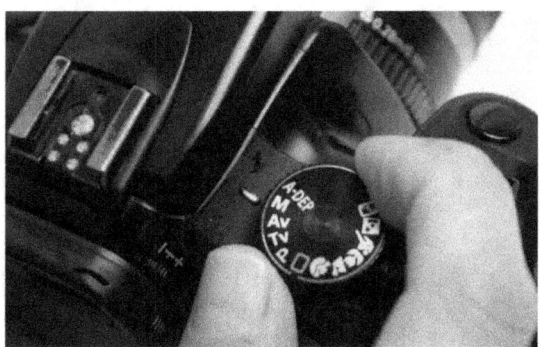

Figure 9: Exploring the Exposure Feature of Cameras

The Exposure Slider for the iPhone 11 Pro makes it possible for users to manually control the camera's

16

exposure, thereby overriding the iPhone's exposure settings.

The exposure slider is generally handy when correcting the brightness of a shot even though you can equally use it to over or underexpose a shot when trying to achieve a specific visual effect.

Filters

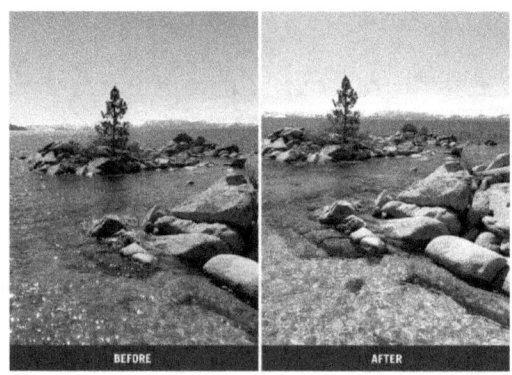

Figure 10: Enhance Photos Using Filter Option

This means the preset filters on the app can be applied even at the point of taking pictures or Live Mode.

Self-Timer

The iPhone 11 Pro comes with the filter option even though inferior to the filters offered by programs like Instagram, it can apply filters in changing the hues in your pictures using the Camera app on the iPhone.

It is time to take a family picture, only that there is no stranger around to help capture the shot. This is an example among many other situations where the self-timer can be used.

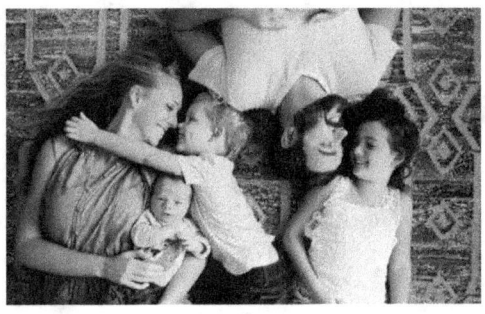

Figure 11: Take Family Pictures using Self Timer

The self-timer feature is one of the options you find at the top right corner of the camera app on the iPhone 11's Pro screen.

Gridline

The use of gridlines when taking pictures is a favorite feature for many people who are unable to take advantage of some of the sophisticated features of the iPhone's camera like composition. Many amateurs use this feature by dividing the frame into a 3 x 3 grid and using the Rule of Thirds to know where to place the subject in the frame as a way of overcoming the challenges associated with the composition feature of the iPhone 11 Pro camera.

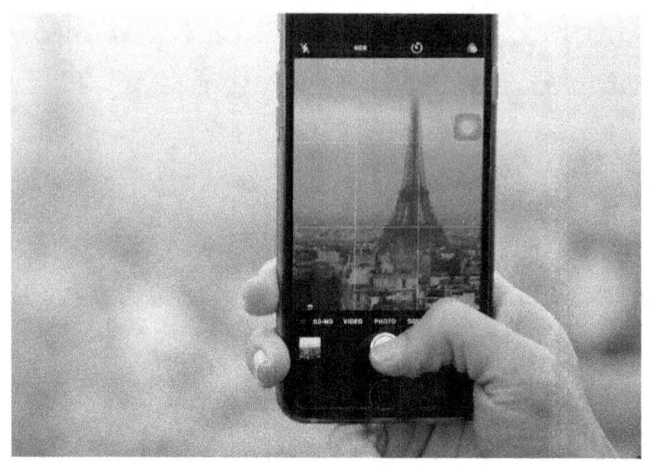

Figure 12: Taking Advantage of Gridlines in Taking Shots

When using grid lines, you only need to position the main subject on any of the lines in the grid intersections.

High Dynamic Range (HDR)

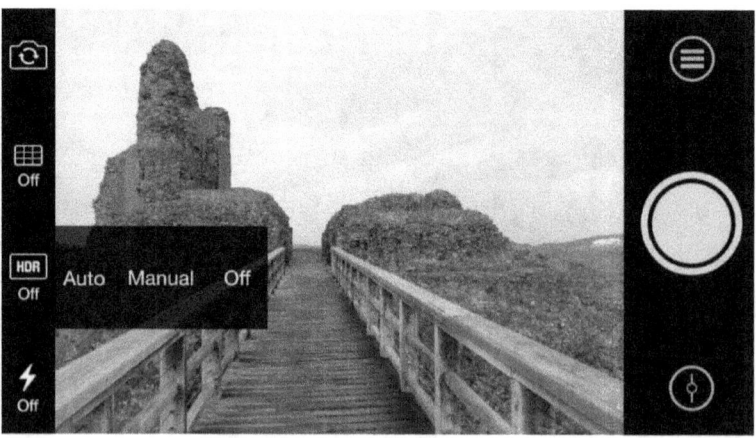

Figure 13: HDR Feature of the iPhone 11 Pro

The HDR is beneficial for capturing shots in very tricky lighting conditions where manual adjustments and automatic settings are unable to control the exposure levels. You will find the HDR useful in high-contrast lightings like sunsets, sunrise, and overcast scenes. By activating the HDR, it prompts the phone to capture three different photos with varying exposure levels, which are then composed together to create a clear image with the right exposure.

Chapter 3

ርጽፀጋርጽፀጋርጽፀጋ

Capturing Photos on iPhone 11 Pro

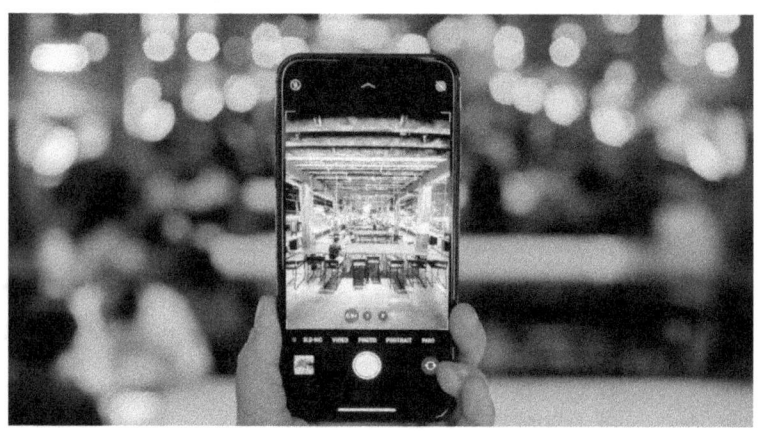

iPhone 11 Pro Camera Modes

Apple's iPhone 11 Pro comes with some changes in the features of the new camera app compared to other iPhones using iOS 13 and later. It comes with new controls, a way to move between the different cameras and other features like quick video and more. This updated camera app interface can display an entire field of view captured by the camera's ultra-wide lens even though when it is the standard wide-angle lens that is being used in taking the photoshoot. Toggling between each of these modes is easily done by simply tapping and swiping relevant sections of the camera app.

To select a mode for shooting, simply swipe left or right across the screen or swipe down or up when holding the phone horizontally. Once a mode is selected, it will appear in yellow while the others will remain white.

The iPhone 11 Pro Camera app has six modes for shooting different photography and video modes. The modes include:

- Time-Lapse
- Slo-Mo
- Video
- Photo
- Portrait
- Pano

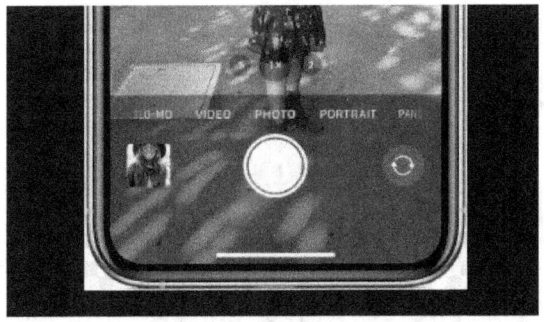

Figure 14: iPhone 11 Pro Photography Modes

Photo Mode

The default mode on the iPhone 11 Pro camera app is usually the Photo mode. This is also probably the most frequently used mode on the iPhone camera app because people tend to take a lot of still pictures with their phones compared to other photographic functions on the phone. It is used to capture normal still images.

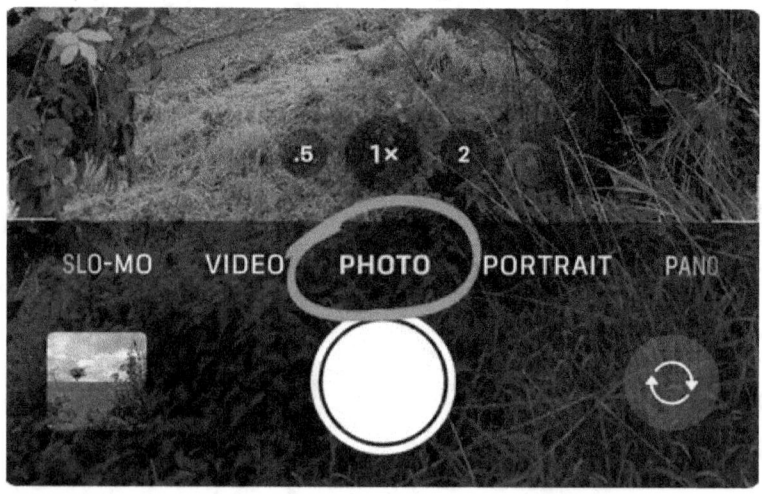

Figure 15: Photo Mode of iPhone 11 Pro

Portrait Mode

To the right of the Photo mode on the iPhone 11 Pro Camera app is the Portrait mode. This feature is a handy one for shooting highly professional portrait photos with the iPhone as well as in creating beautiful background blur behind photoshoots.

23

Compared to the iPhone 7 Plus, 8 Plus, X, XS, XS Max, and iPhone XR which only allowed the use of their 2x telephoto camera when taking a portrait mode photo, the iPhone 11 Pro enables users to choose between the wide and telephoto lens for their portrait mode shots.

As expected, each of these modes produces an effect that is different from the other with the wide camera able to take better portrait photos in low light compared to the other camera because of its faster f/1.8 aperture.

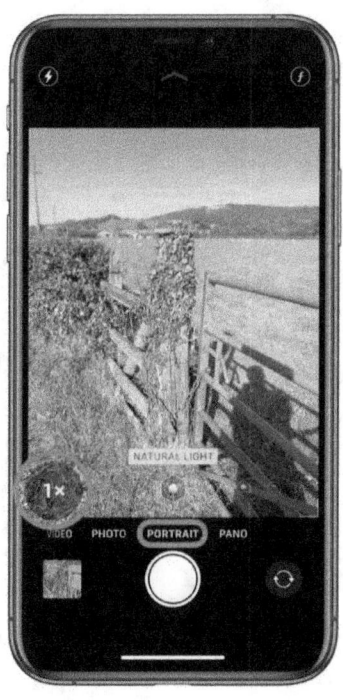

Figure 16: Portrait Mode of iPhone 11 Pro

Portrait mode is perfect for shooting professional-looking portrait photos.

Pano Mode

Next to the portrait mode is the Pano mode on the right. This mode is used to capture super-wide landscapes and cityscape pictures, including photos that are panoramic in order to capture more of the scenes.

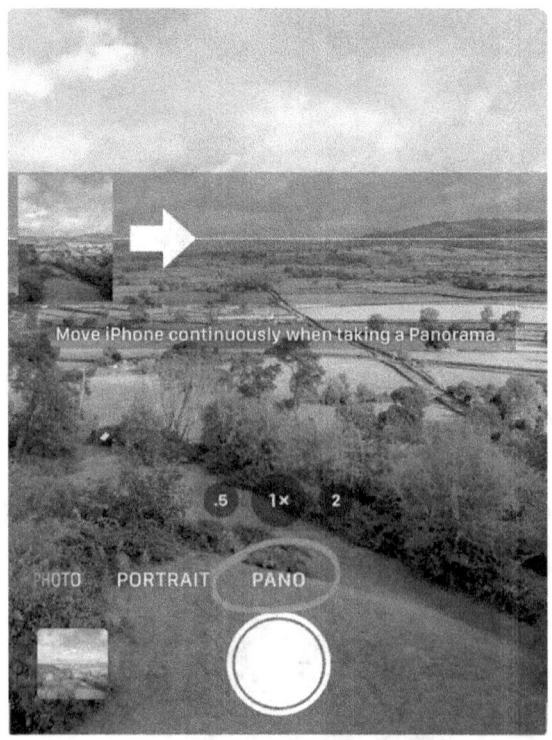

Figure 17: Pano Mode of iPhone 11 Pro

To use the Pano mode, you first tap the shutter button and then start moving the iPhone across the scene in the direction indicated by the arrow. As soon as you capture the parts of the scene you want to be captured, you can then tap the shutter button again to complete the shooting process.

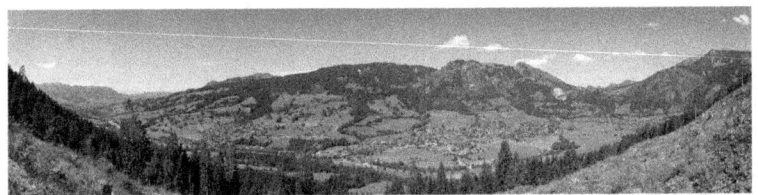

Figure 18: Photoshoot from Pano Mode

Video Mode

To the immediate left of the photo mode on the camera app is the video mode. This mode is used in the shooting of high-quality video footage. To use this feature, you start by tapping the red Record button to begin recording a video and tapping it again to stop its recording.

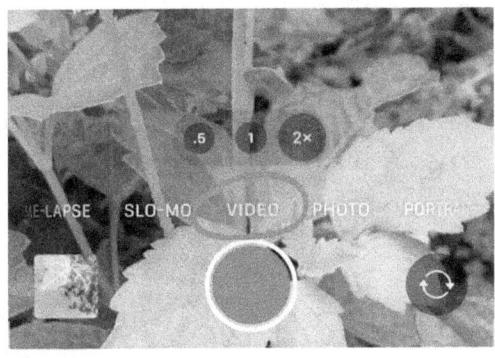

Figure 19: iPhone 11 Pro Video Mode

Slo-Mo Mode

Next to the video mode is the Slo-Mo mode used in capturing amazing slow-motion videos of fast-moving subjects like someone or an object running, flying, jumping, or moving.

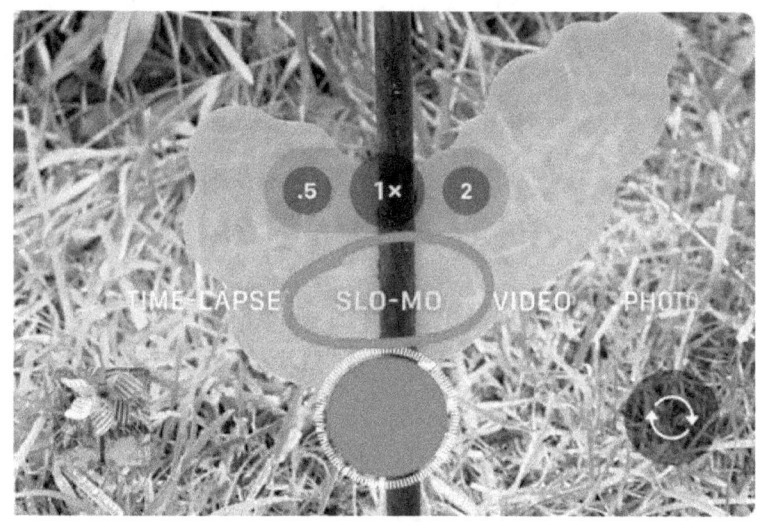

Figure 20: iPhone 11 Pro Slo-Mo Mode

As is common with other camera modes, you also have to tap the red Record button to begin recording a So-Mo and another tap to stop its recording.

Time-Lapse Mode

Another essential camera mode of the iPhone 11 Pro camera app is the Time-Lapse Mode. This mode performs a function that is opposite of the Slo-Mo. It does this by creating a sped-up time-lapse video.

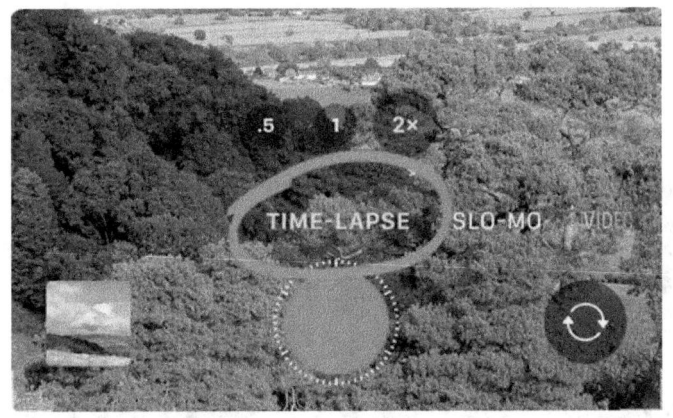

Figure 21: Time-Lapse Mode

For Time-lapse, you also have to tap the red Record button to begin recording your time-lapse. To end the recording, all you have to do is to tap it again.

This feature is a fantastic way of hastening up slow-moving scenes like burning candles, clouds, or sunset.

Exploring The iPhone 11 Pro Lenses

The iPhone 11 Pro has three rear-facing lenses that include the Wide lens, an Ultra-Wide lens, and the telephoto lens, with each of them having different functions and specific uses. The Wide Lens is the iPhone 11 Pro's standard lens and has a relatively wide angle for viewing. Compared to the wide lens, the ultra-Wide lens gives users a much wider view field that users can use in capturing a lot more of any given scene, which makes it very useful in capturing wide architectural landscapes and nature pictures. It's equally great for capturing group

28

pictures when you want more people to fit into the frame as well as interior shots where you want more parts of the scene captured.

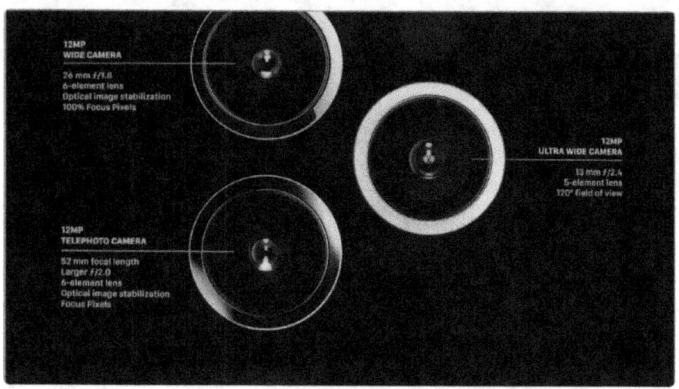

Figure 22: iPhone 11 Pro Camera Lenses

The Telephoto lens, on the other hand, is beneficial for shots you want to zoom in to get a closer view. It is ideal for situations where you are unable to physically get close to the subject you want to capture.

To compare the images from the different types of lenses, you will need to take pictures with the different lenses and to see the output of each of them.

Switching Between the Lenses

Switching between iPhone camera lenses is as easy as simply tapping the Zoom icons at the bottom of the viewfinder.

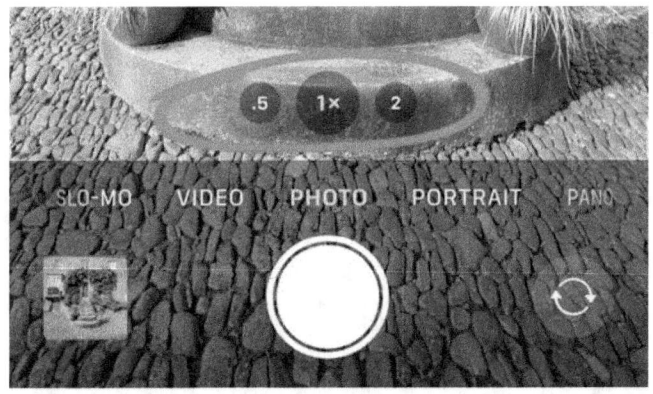

Figure 23: Wide Angle, Ultra-Wide and Telephoto Lenses Selection

Switching to the Standard Wide-Angle Lens

To use the standard wide lens on any of the applicable modes like the photo mode, video mode, or pano mode, you simply tap the 1x under the viewfinder. Usually, this will be the default mode of the camera app.

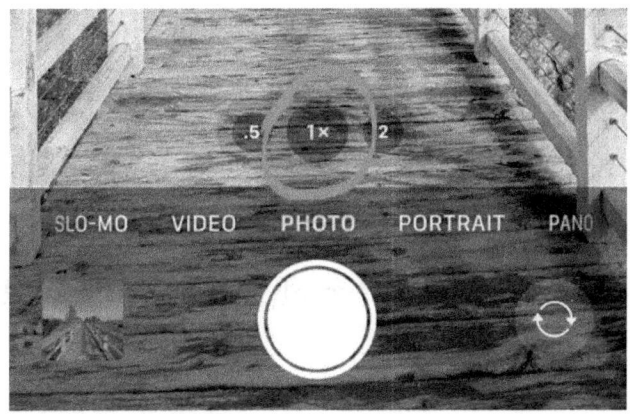

Figure 24: Standard Wide-Angle Lens Selection

Switching to the Ultra-Wide-Angle Lens

The ultra-wide-angle lens is useful for expanding the field of view of the camera for the scene where pictures are to be shot. To switch to the Ultra-Wide lens, simply tap the 0.5x.

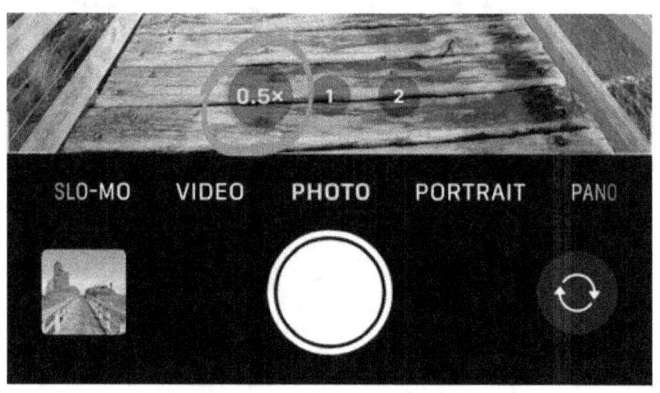

Figure 25: Ultra-Wide-Angle Lens Selection

Switching to the Telephoto Lens

The telephoto lens is useful in narrowing down the field of view of the camera lens by zooming in on the subject that the iPhone 11 Pro and 11 Pro Max want to shoot. The telephoto lens is the major difference between the iPhone 11 and iPhone 11 Pro. To switch the iPhone 11 Pro to the telephoto lens, simply tap the 2x icon below the viewfinder.

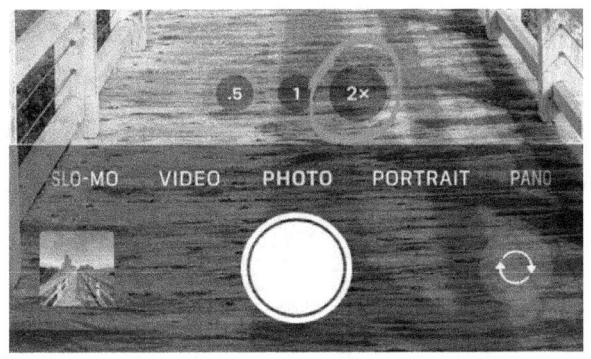

Figure 26: Telephoto Lens Selection

When you're using the 1x Wide lens or 2x Telephoto lens to shoot a scene, it will display a wider view of the scene outside of the frame. This will enable you to have an idea of what can be captured if you were to zoom out.

You can also get the zoom wheel to appear by holding down on any of the Zoom (0.5x, 1x, or 2x) icons.

The zoom wheel is very useful in choosing granular values different from the three fixed standard values and also shows the equivalent focal length in a 35mm film. The zoom wheel allows you to zoom anywhere from 0.5x to 10x. By dragging the wheel towards the left or right, transiting between the different zoom levels can be achieved. For a lot of people, using the standard values of 0.5x, 1x and 2x is usually sufficient for them because any zoom outside these three standard values will force the iPhone 11 Pro camera to use its digital zoom feature which tends to result in much more inferior image quality that does not do enough justice to the iPhone 11 Pro camera capabilities. The fixed focal length values of 0.5x, 1x, and 2x built-into the cameras make use of the full optical quality of the three iPhone 11 Pro's lenses to produce high-quality images.

Fine Tuning the zoom in and Out

The iPhone 11 Pro gives users an added advantage of making use of all the three 12 megapixels lenses that it comes with, including their respective zoom levels.

The control of the iPhone 11 Pro Camera's zoom is different from other previous versions. On the iPhone, you will find two (0.5x and 1x) buttons that you can tap, whereas the iPhone 11 Pro has a third button for its 2x zoom.

The iPhone 11 Pro uses 1x for the default camera wide lens, whereas the ultra-wide camera uses the 0.5x option from the possible three options available when you attempt using the zoom.

To zoom on the iPhone 11 Pro

- Tap on the camera app to open it
- Select either the 0.5x, 1x or the 2x buttons on the camera app to jump to that zoom level or you can tap and hold any of the options to open up the zoom wheel

- Drag the dial that appears so that you can transition between the other cameras and zoom more smoothly

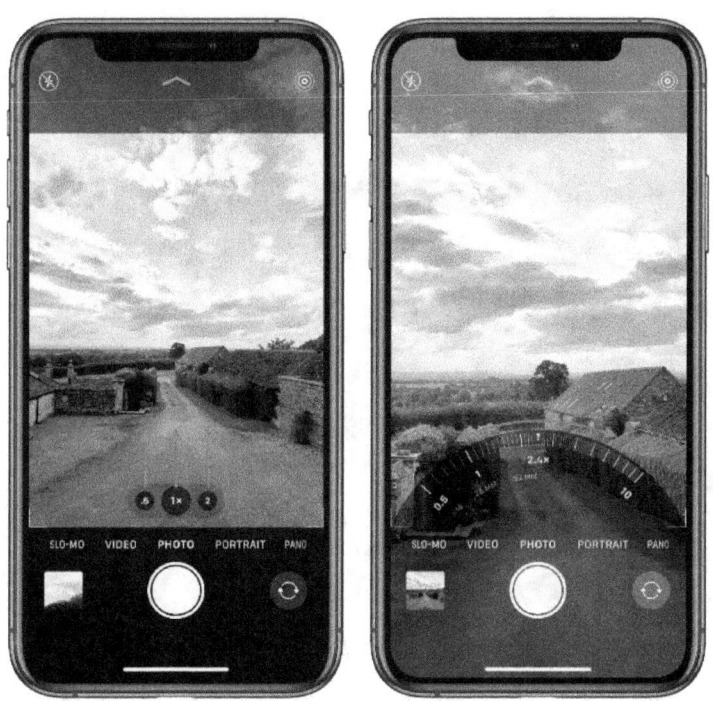

Figure 27: Zooming Images Using Presets or Zoom Wheel

You use this option to select intermediate zoom levels rather than specific values and also expose the equivalent focal length in 35mm film.

If you have used any of the custom zoom levels, it is possible to move back to 1x by just pressing the center button.

Another way to Operate the Zoom Feature

- Tap the camera app to launch the app
- Pinch and zoom with two of your fingers on the screen and adjust the zoom
- Switch between the lenses and select your preferred one

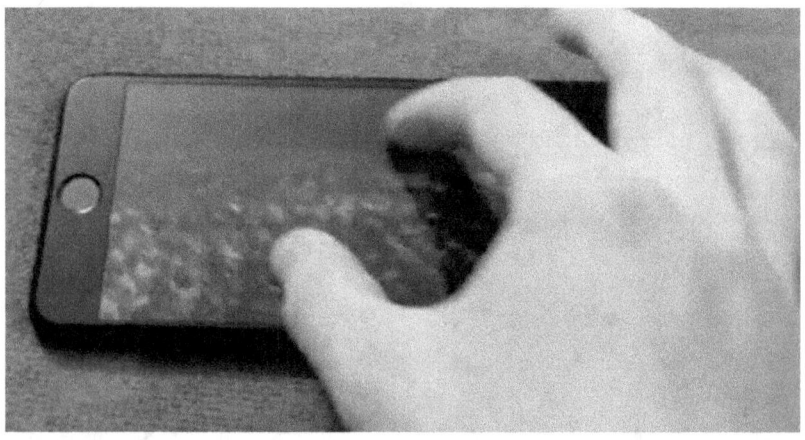

Figure 28: Zooming by Pinching with Two Fingers

NB: This option does not open the focal length wheel

You can return to the 1x zoom at any time by pressing the center button if you have previously changed to a custom zoom level when playing around with the zoom feature.

Zoom Out Photos After Shooting

The iPhone 11 Pro also has a hidden feature that is possible because of the ultrawide camera, that is the possibility of zooming out on a photo captured by any of the other two lenses to get a wider picture frame after you've taken it. With this feature, more people who were originally not captured in a group photograph can be included because the ultra-wide pictures tend to keep a copy of every shot taken so that you can bring such persons initially missed back into the shot using the crop tool on the Photos app.

Using the Volume Buttons as a Shutter

You can take a picture with the iPhone 11 Pro using the volume button instead of the shutter button. As with many things on the iPhone 11 Pro, this is essentially simple to do.

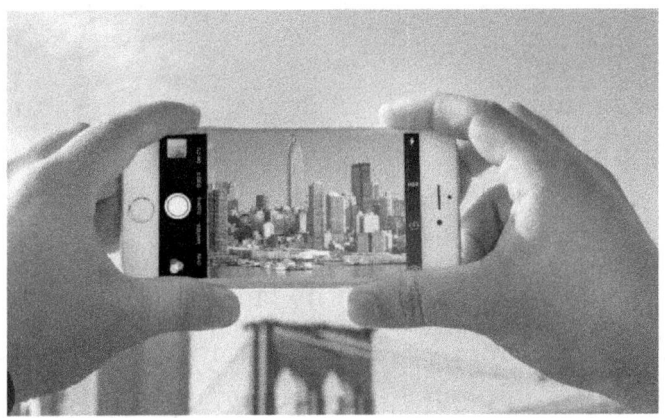

Figure 29: Taking a Picture with the Volume Button

- Tap Camera app to launch it
- Focus the camera on the subject you want to take

- Tap the up-volume button to take a picture

Taking Pictures with the Rear Cameras

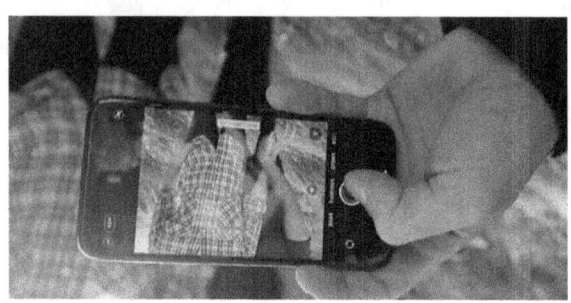

Figure 30: Capture Important Moments with the iPhone 11 Pro

- Launch the Camera app by tapping on it. The default mode when you launch the Camera app will be the Photo mode
- Direct the camera to focus on the subject whose picture is to be taken
- When the subject is in focus, tap the shutter to snap the picture

How to Record Videos

- Launch the Camera app by tapping on it.
- Change from the default Photo mode to Video mode by tapping on the video option beside the photo option above the shutter button

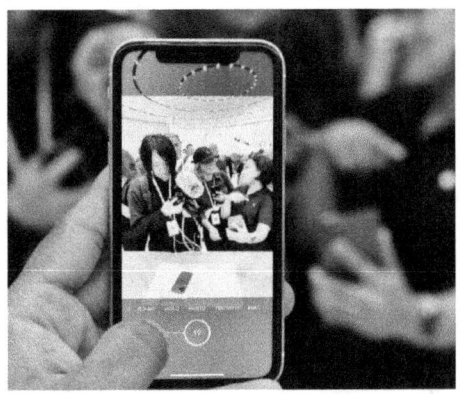

Figure 31: Capture Important Moments Using the Video Recorder

- Tap the Record button to start the recording
- Tap the Record button again to stop recording when done

Recording a Video Between Photos Using QuickTake

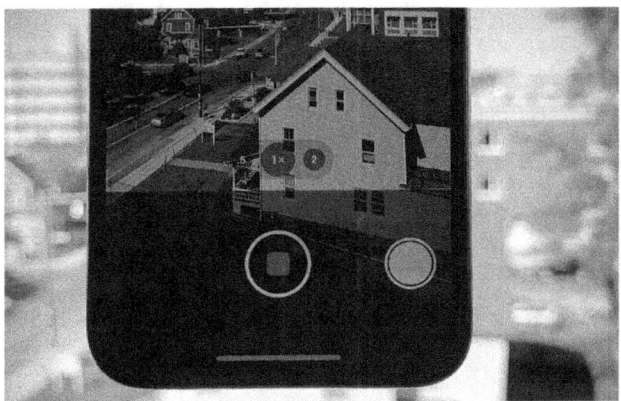

Figure 32: Switching Quickly from Still Pictures to Video Recording

If you have ever wished there was a way to instantly switch from capturing a still picture to start recording a video without having to change modes just like in a

Snapchat story or Instagram story, then the QuickTake feature is for you. To achieve that on older iPhones will typically involve switching to Video mode and pressing the shutter button to begin recording. On the iPhone 11 Pro, you can shoot a video and still stay in Photo mode.

This feature is very simple to activate and use, although slightly different from the way lower versions of the iPhone 11 Pro achieve it. QuickTake can be used on both front and rear cameras, even though users have to pay attention to the aspect ratio. QuickTake will always inherit the aspect ratio of the photograph being taken, so a photograph set to 4:3 will use that same setting for the QuickTake. If you prefer your video to be 16:9 instead, you will need to set the photo aspect ratio accordingly. To record with the QuickTake, pay attention to the following steps.

- Hold the shutter button to begin recording the QuickTake video while still in the Photo mode. The shutter button will turn red. And you'll see the video timer at the top of the screen.
- Remove your hands from the shutter to stop the QuickTake video recording, and you can continue taking photos.

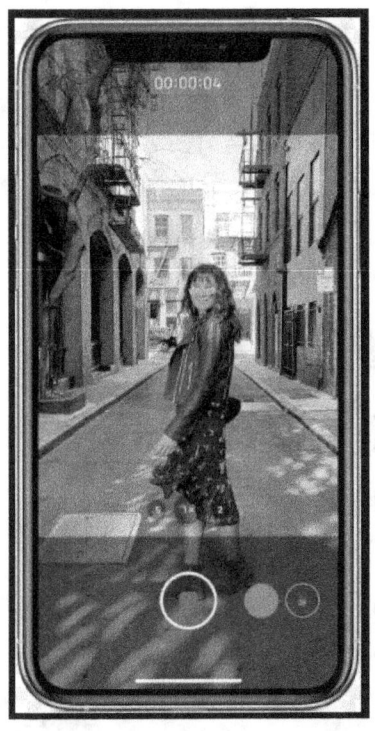

Figure 33: QuickTake Timer

To release your hands to keep capturing still pictures or performing other activities, it is better to lock the QuickTake while the video recording is ongoing.

- To achieve this, slide the Shutter button to the right of the screen to expose both the record and shutter buttons below the frame
- When you lock the video recording, a white shutter button appears at the bottom right corner of the screen. The shutter button can then be used to

continue taking still images, while the QuickTake video recording is still ongoing.

- The Record button can be used to stop the ongoing recording by simply tapping it.

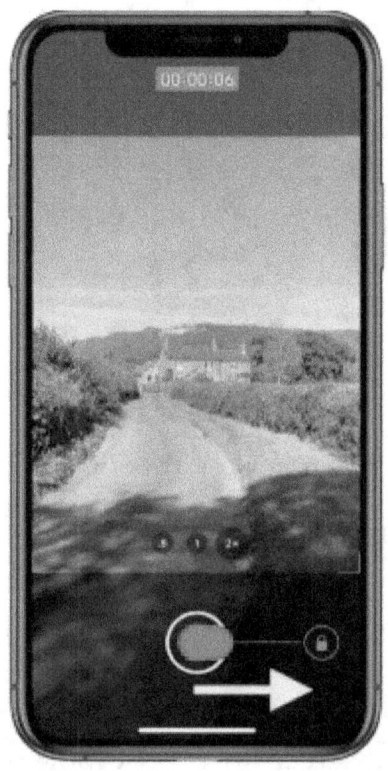

Figure 34: Locking the QuickTake Video

This is a really cool feature that allows users to both shoot videos and photos at the same time. It is important to note that the resolution of the images can be slightly lower than normal, but nowhere near being a poor-quality image.

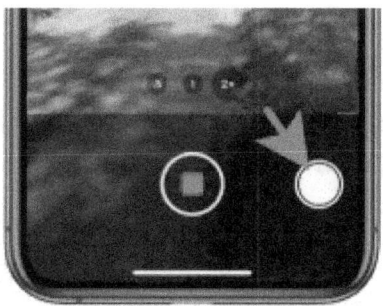

Figure 35: White Shutter Button to Continue Pictures

Taking Burst Photos

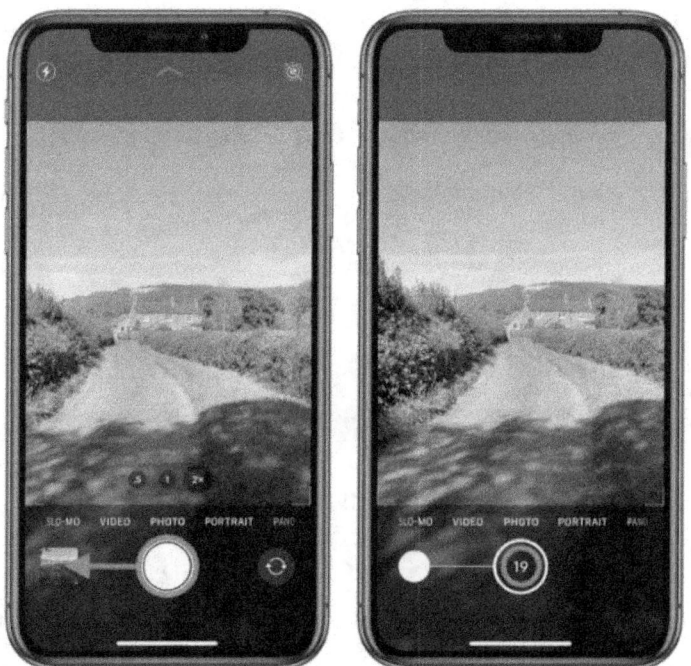

Figure 36: Using the Burst Features of the iPhone 11 Pro

Imagine you want a precise picture of you taken midair when you leap off the ground and want the timing to be gotten right so that the image comes out crisp and not blurry, or you want to take a shot of you running, or a picture of a moving vehicle, previous versions of the iPhone have customarily used the burst function to achieve this. The burst mode is a fantastic iPhone tool for capturing subjects that are in motion. So, if you have difficulty shooting moving objects and you know it can be a struggle to press the shutter button at the precise moment this burst mode feature is definitely for you.

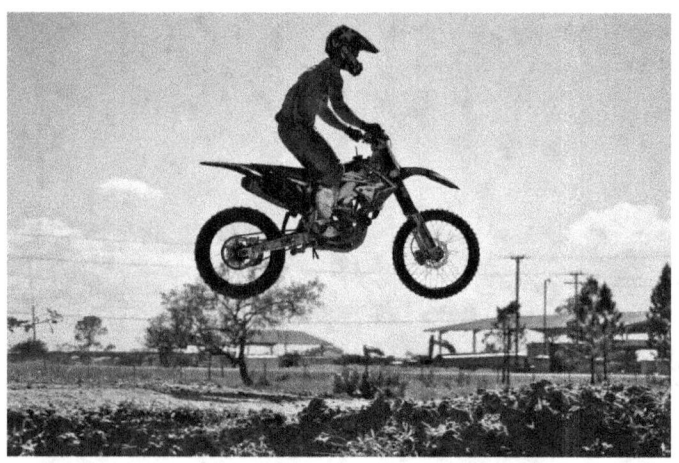

Figure 37: Capture Image Mid Air with Burst Feature

In earlier versions of the iPhone that also had the burst function like the iPhone 11 Pro, you only needed to press and hold the shutter button, and the device will keep capturing the pictures for as long as the finger remains on the screen.

Well, for the new iPhone 11 Pro, that function is now used for the QuickTake function. In this recent release, the burst currently requires some more steps to achieve compared to just holding the shutter in the photo mode of previous versions. When you take a shot in burst mode, multiple photos are taken every second to capture the subject as it moves across the scene until you release your finger so that you are able to select the best shot from the burst with the option to discard the others. The number of photos taken within the burst is indicated by the number inside the shutter.

To take a burst on the iPhone 11 Pro, follow these simple steps.

- Launch the Camera app on your iPhone
- Press on the shutter button
- Then quickly swipe to the left towards the photo's stack of thumbnails if you are taking a vertical photo or swipe down for horizontal photos

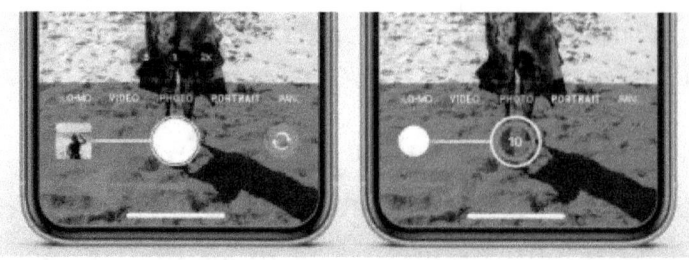

Figure 38: Shooting a Burst Photo

Ensure the shutter button is not red. If it is red, that means you may have held your finger too long on the shutter causing the phone to think you want to record a video. It that is the case, you have to start all over.

If you did it correctly, the shutter cycle would move in the direction of your finger to indicate the starting of the burst. To end the burst, simply remove your finger from the screen.

When the burst photo shooting has been completed, you can then open the burst thumbnail in the Photos app. The burst photos can be identified from the thumbnail by their stacked images. It is from there that you now tap and select the Relevant you want to keep. Tap Done when through to keep only the selected photos. The selected pictures are then saved to your photo library, and the others deleted.

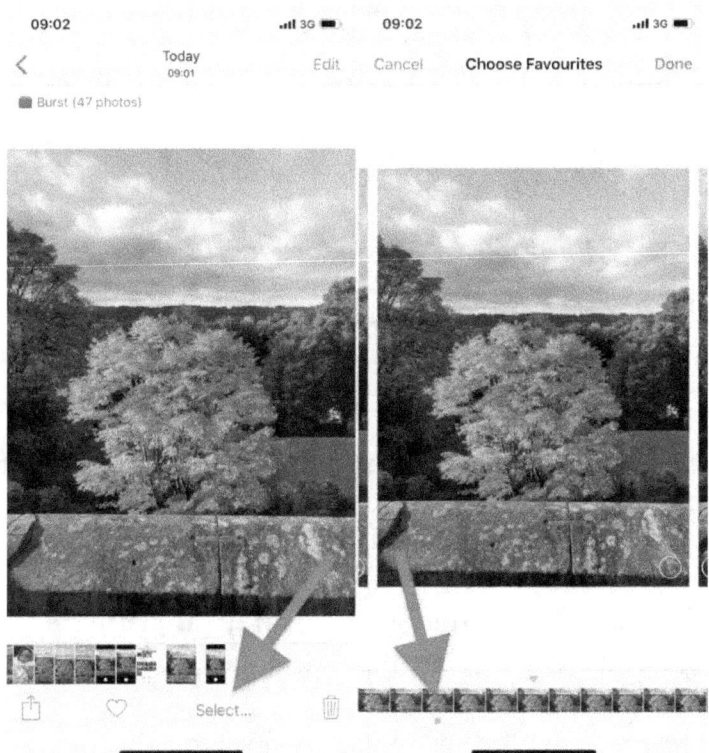

Figure 39: Burst Mode Picture Selection

Setting Up Photo Capture Outside of the Frame

Capturing images outside a photo frame with the ultra-wide uses a function referred to as composition. Composition is an important feature that differentiates a well-taken picture from an ordinary snapshot. If, for example, you want to take a shot, but there are persons on the edge of the frame not captured, rather than zoom in, you can instead recover a slightly wider field of view by utilizing the cameras on the iPhone 11 Pro by turning

46

on the composition setting. To set the phone to be able to take pictures outside the frame, you can follow these steps.

- Tap to launch the Settings App on your iPhone
- Select and tap Camera
- Toggle the switch close to the Photos Capture Outside the Frame and Videos Capture Outside the Frame to switch on the iPhone's function of being able to capture images and videos outside the current frame
- Next, tap the switch beside Auto Apply Adjustment so that composition adjustments can be applied to any of your photoshoots

It is noteworthy to know that enabling and disabling this function can only be done by going into the Settings app and not the Camera app. So, go to Settings -> Camera -> Composition, where you can set the three toggles. You will notice that separate toggles are used to control the outside the frame switches for photos and videos and another switch for Auto-Apply Adjustments.

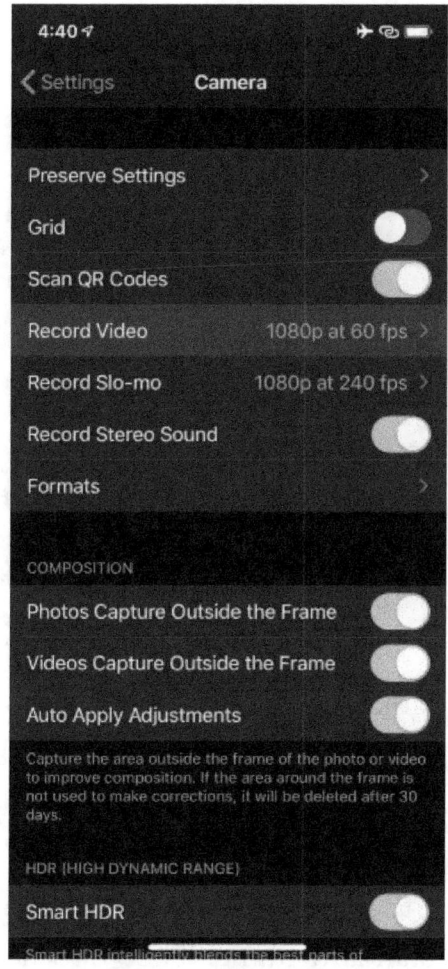

Figure 40: Configuring Composition on the iPhone 11 Pro

A valuable note about this feature is that when you capture photos or videos outside the standard frame of your camera, you will be required to save the images using Apple's higher efficient HEIC and HEVC image instead of JPG.

Taking Advantage of Outside the Frame

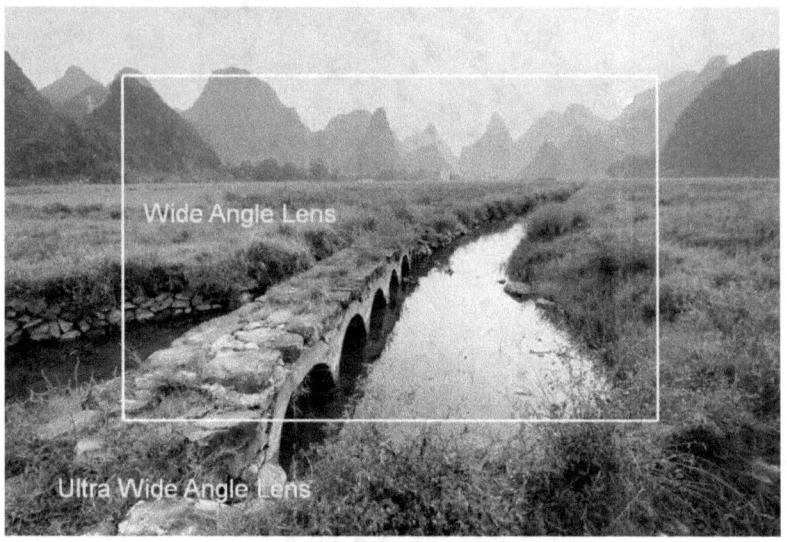

Figure 41: Utilizing the Ultra and Wide-angle-lens

While it is possible to use the wide-angle shot when taking a picture, it is also sometimes possible to have taken a picture around the active viewfinder, only to discover when you want to edit or use the image that some aspect of the background was cut out and not captured in the standard frame. The good news is that if you have set the outside the frame feature in the iPhone settings, then you can nevertheless have access to the ultra-wide-angle shot because the iPhone ensures that it takes more than one shot when a picture is being taken. Therefore, if you took a photo, but a person on the edge of the frame isn't captured, you can then edit the photo by zooming out to see a wider shot of the image which may now have the person that was left out in the standard frame because the ultra-wide lens would have also taken a copy of the picture. It should be noted that this can only happen if you turned on Photo Capture Outside the Frame the phone's composition setting and works for both photos and videos. To take advantage of this feature, you can follow the simple steps below.

- Tap to launch the Photos app on your iPhone 11 Pro
- Tap to open the video or photo you want to edit
- Tap Edit. If the picture has data from outside the frame that can be edited, you will notice a rangefinder icon with a star
- Use the crop tool to extend the edges surrounding the present frame to expose more parts of the photo or videos
- You can equally use the Auto-Apply to do this automatically for situations where the app can detect faces or subjects that were not captured
- Tap Done after the edit

If you capture images outside the standard frame, you have to note these pictures can get deleted after 30 days if they are unused within that time frame even though the image from the standard lens can nonetheless exist long after the picture had been taken.

Although this feature is simple to use, many users sometimes find it confusing to use. Some captured pictures sometimes do not display other aspects of the photos when zoomed in, even though the square star that is used to indicate that more information exists outside the frame.

It turns out that there are two different ways of accessing the information captured outside the frame. However, if trying to zoom out on a photo doesn't work, you can try selecting the Crop tool as before, then tap on the three-dot icon at the top right corner and then tap Use Content Outside the Frame. For photos that have previously been cropped and straightened, there is likely to be a warning message that your previous cropping is about to be reset, tap to accept the warning so that you are now able to edit the ultrawide shot.

Chapter 4

Manipulating Images on iPhone 11 Pro

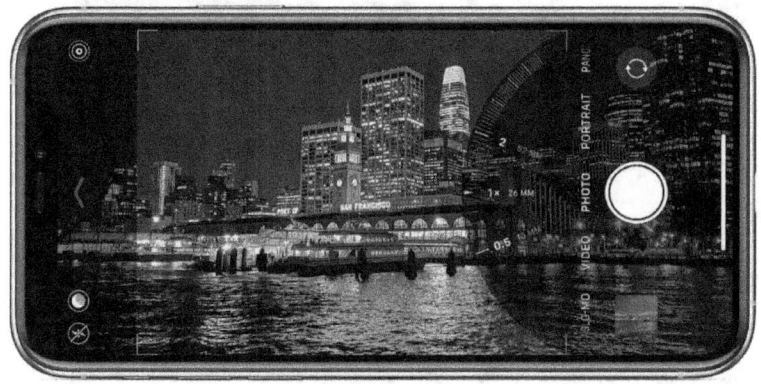

For those who prefer to use the iPhone's native app in editing photos rather than utilizing expensive editing programs like Photoshop, the instructions below are useful. The iPhone 11 Pro has powerful photo editing tools that can be used to edit photos for cropping, filtering, adjusting color balance and other simple essential functions.

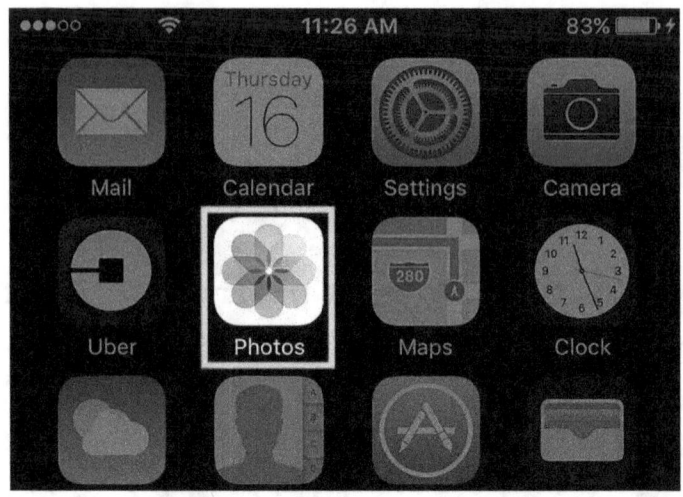

Figure 42: iPhone Photos App

Editing a Photo or Video

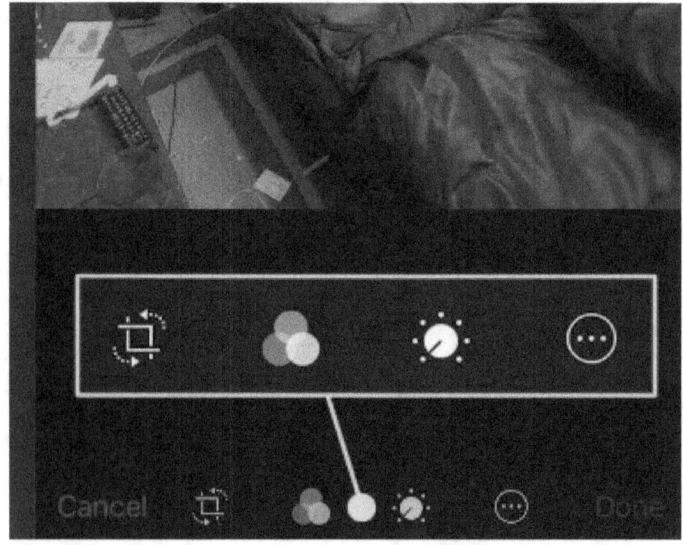

Figure 43: Locating the Edit Button on the Photos App

- Tap the Photos app to launch it

- Tap the photo or video thumbnail you intend to edit to open it
- Tap Edit, then swipe left below the photo to view the buttons for editing effects like crop, brilliance, highlights, and exposure.
- Tap a button and then drag the slider to make the changes required
- The outline displayed around the button is used to indicate the effects of the adjustments made as they either increase or decrease

Comparing the Before and After Effects of Photo Edits

With the Photos app still opened, after the changes have been applied, you can see the effects of your actions on the subject by performing the following steps.

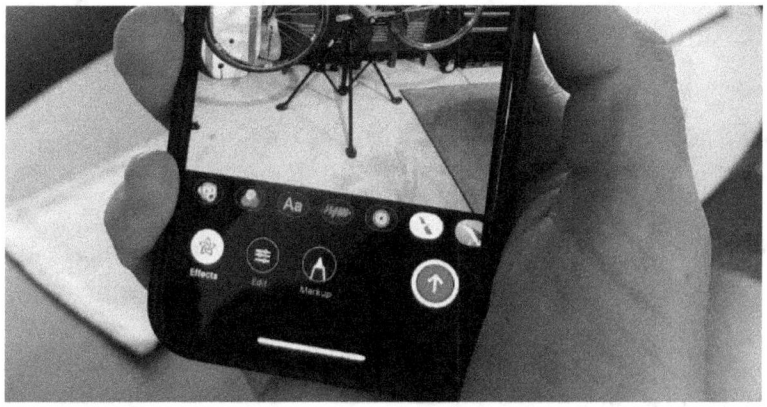

Figure 44: Locating the Effects Button on the Photos App

- Tap the effect button to show the before effects shots of the photo and the aftereffect shots of the picture.
- Tap the photo to toggle from the original version of the picture to the edited version
- Tap Done to accept the changes and Cancel to discard the changes

Take Screenshots

Taking screenshots on the iPhone 11 Pro is one feature that many users find very useful because it allows them to document activities or messages on the phone for future references. To do that, you have to follow these simple steps.

- Press and hold the Volume up button with the Side button at the same time before releasing them quickly.
- The thumbnail of your screenshot will appear at the lower-left corner of your screen
- Tap that thumbnail to effect minor changes and edits
- To share the screenshot, press and hold the thumbnail

- However, if you are unsatisfied with it and perhaps want to discard it, you can swipe it to the left of the screen to do so, otherwise, you can save it

Knowing the Different Cropping Options

Many users of the iPhone 11 Pro cameras are likely to be social media savvy and may not want to be restricted in terms of the photo ratio or sizes and want to be able to adjust pictures after they have been taken. Fortunately, the iPhone 11 Pro allows that to happen.

- Tap to open the iPhone 11's Pro Photos app
- Tap a photo or video thumbnail of what you desire to edit
- Tap Edit and select the crop tool, you can identify it by its square icon with arrows surrounding it

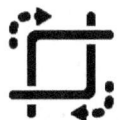

- To crop manually, drag the corners of the rectangle surrounding it by closing in on the areas of the photo you want to keep. You can also pinch the picture and drag to obtain the corresponding effect
- To crop to a standard preset ratio, tap the preset button, and select any of the preset options like the Square, 5:4, 3:2, 5:3,4:3, and 8:10. You can use 16:9

and 7:5 for panoramic photos even though 1:1 is more popular with Instagram users

- To rotate an image, tap the rounded square with a rotating arrow on top to rotate the photo by 90 degrees
- Select the flip button to flip the image horizontally when you want to flip an image around
- Tap Done to save changes and Cancel to discard changes.

Straightening and Adjusting Perspective

- Tap the Photos app to launch it
- Tap a photo or video thumbnail of what you desire to edit
- Tap Edit followed by the crop button
- Select an effect button for straightening and adjusting the horizontal and vertical perspective
- For photos captured by the ultra-wide camera, aspects of the picture outside the frame can be automatically used to make changes to alignments and perspective. A blue Auto icon that appears above the photo is used to indicate an automatic adjustment was applied
- Use the slider to adjust the effect by sliding across the slider

- Watch the displayed yellow outline around the button to monitor the effectiveness of your adjustments on the photo
- Tap the button to switch between the original and the edited effect to observe the impact of your changes
- Tap Done to save your changes or Cancel to discard your change

Applying Filter Effects

- Tap to launch the Photos app
- Tap a photo or video thumbnail to open the photo you want to edit
- Tap Edit followed by the filter button 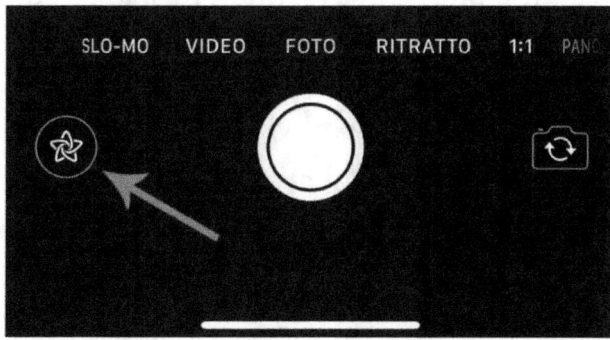 (three cycles arranged in a triangular format) to apply any of the filters you want

Figure 45: Selecting Options on the Camera App

- Tap to select a filter and use the slider to adjust the effect of the filter
- Tap the photo to switch between the original and edited photo to monitor the differences so far
- Tap Done when satisfied with the outcome and Cancel to discard the changes

Marking Up a Photo

- Tap the Photos app to open it
- Tap a photo you want to put annotations on
- Tap edit and tap the three dots at the top
- Select Markup
- Use the different available drawing tools and colors to annotate the photo
- Tap the plus sign to add more shapes and text

Trimming a Video

If you have a video to send via Messages or Mail but find that it is too long to send at once, you may want to only send some parts of the video instead. To do that, you can use the trim function to start and stop the video timing when you want to make the video shorter than the original version without using iMovie.

- Tap the Photos app to open it

- Tap the video thumbnail of the video you want to edit
- Tap Edit and drag either end of the frame viewer
- Release when satisfied with the trim
- Tap Done to accept changes or Cancel to discard

Reverting to an Original Photo or Video

Even after editing and saving the changes in a photo, you can revert to the original image by adopting these simple steps.

- Tap the Photo's App to launch it
- Tap the Photo or Video thumbnail to open the photo that was edited
- Tap Edit followed by Revert
- Select Revert to Original

Changing the Aspect Ratio

Unlike previous versions of the iPhone, where users could choose from 4:3 aspect ratio (rectangle) or the 1:1 aspect ratio (Square), the iPhone 11 Pro groups the ratio settings into a single-mode, which also includes the new 16:9 aspect ratio. To change the aspect ratio, you can follow the steps below.

- Launch the Camera app

- Swipe up the screen to expose more of the Camera settings
- Tap the aspect ratio button (usually 4:3 by default)
- Select any of the available options to make it the new aspect ratio

Shooting with the Ultra-Wide Lens

- It is easy to shoot with the iPhone ultra-wide lens
- Tap to open the Camera app
- Tap the 1x button to switch over to the 0.5x ultra-wide lens
- You can now take your picture

Chapter 5

CBEOCBEOCBEO

Additional Controls on the Camera App

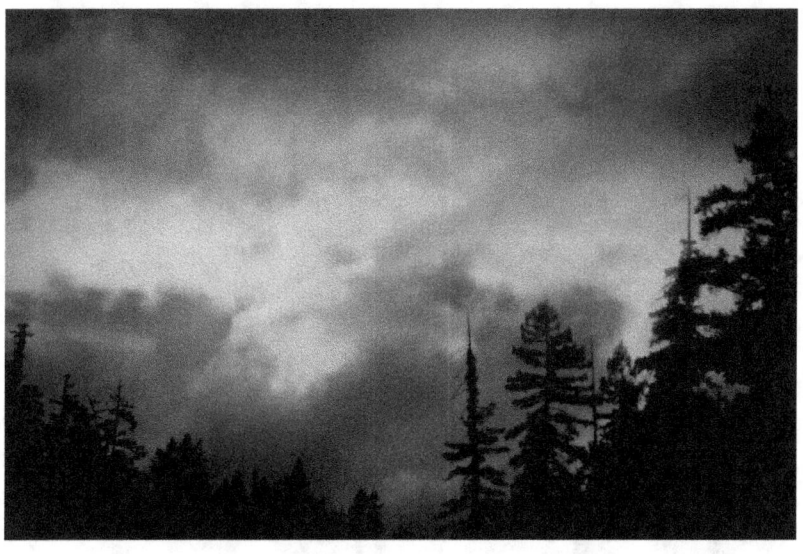

The iPhone 11 Pro Camera comes with many other hidden controls and settings that a user can manipulate. Whenever you notice a triangular arrow pointing upwards, you can swipe it up on the viewfinder to expose a new set of controls. Other controls like options for flash, night mode, live photos, and a few others are possible within these extra functions.

Taking a Selfie

The iPhone 11 Pro comes with a 12-megapixel front-facing camera even though it does not always utilize the full 12 megapixels for every selfie taken. By holding the iPhone 11 Pro vertically, the image sensor can zoom in and take a 7-megapixel selfie, whereas tapping the expand button can cause the phone to zoom out and use the full 12-megapixel camera when taking a shot.

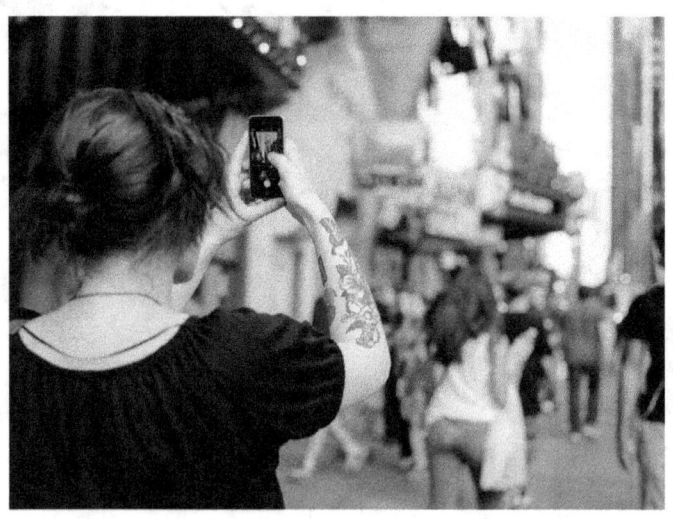

Figure 46: Never a Dull Moment with the Selfie

However, if the iPhone 11 Pro is rotated horizontally for a selfie or slofie, the camera will zoom out automatically for the 12-megapixel selfie, probably because it assumes such a position is usually adopted when there are many people to fit in on the shot or capture a much larger scene. You equally have the option to zoom in to get a 7-megapixel shot instead.

- To take a selfie, you can use the front-facing camera in Photo mode
- Tap the perspective flip button to activate the front-facing camera
- Hold the phone so that it is in your front
- Tap the arrows inside the frame to increase the field of view to capture more objects within the frame
- Tap the shutter button to capture the shot. You can equally use the volume button in capturing the shot

Taking a Slofie

The TrueDepth camera on the iPhone 11 Pro front-facing camera allows it to be able to capture 120 fps slo-mo videos, which opens up a new feature that Apple refers to as "Slofies." Slofies are slow-motion similar to the slo-mo videos available from the rear-facing camera in prior iPhones only that on the iPhone 11 Pro comes from the front-facing cameras.

To take a slofie, you can use the front-facing camera in Photo mode;

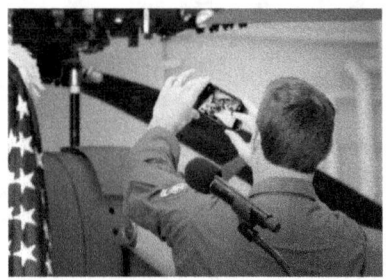

Figure 47: Capture Great Moments with iPhone Slo-Mo Slofie Features

- Tap the perspective flip button to activate the front-facing camera
- Hold the phone so that it is in your front
- Tap the arrows inside the frame to increase the field of view to capture more objects within the frame
- Swipe the visible dial wheel to the right until you reach the slo-mo feature
- Press the shutter to take the slofie

Switching Between Close and Wide-Angle Selfies

- Tap the Camera app to Open it
- Tap the perspective flip button on the screen to toggle between the front-facing and rear camera
- To manually switch between close and wide-angle selfies, tap the arrow button

- To automatically switch between close and wide-angle selfies, you can rotate the iPhone to one side of the phone

Utilizing the Night Mode

Smartphones typically suffer when trying to take pictures in poorly lit circumstances, which is why computational photography comes to the rescue.

Google came up with its own solution and named it Google's Night Sight, similar to what Apple has called Night Mode on its 2019 release of iPhones, including the iPhone 11 Pro. Apple's own low-light photo shooting mode solution combines a mix of hardware and software in getting the phone's photos to be significantly enhanced in dark conditions.

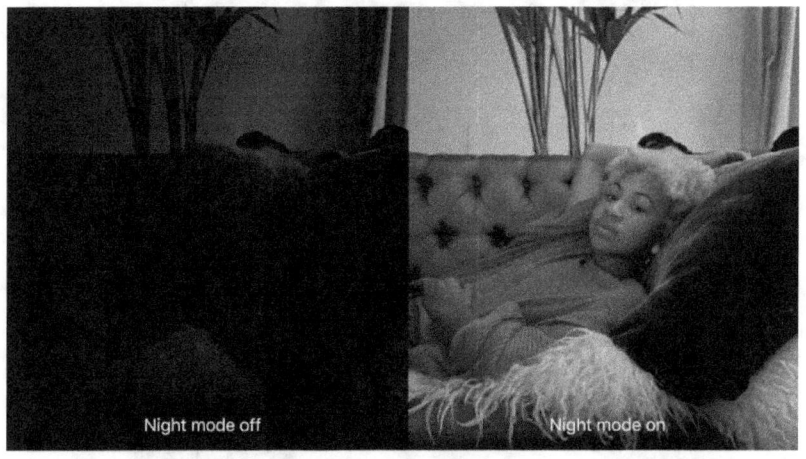

Figure 48: Images With and Without the Night Mode

Apple makes use of computational machine learning in Night Mode by taking multiple shots with different formats, which are then fused together intelligently to create visible images irrespective of how dark it is.

The night mode is extremely useful in capturing images in conditions considered to be low lights to produce images with incredible detail and color. Apple has designed the use of its night mode to be triggered on its own as soon as the iPhone determines that the available light is not sufficient. Once on Night Mode, a yellow half-moon icon will show up next to the arrow button to indicate that the Night Mode is active. Night Mode will allow you to take photos in low lighting without you needing to make use of flash.

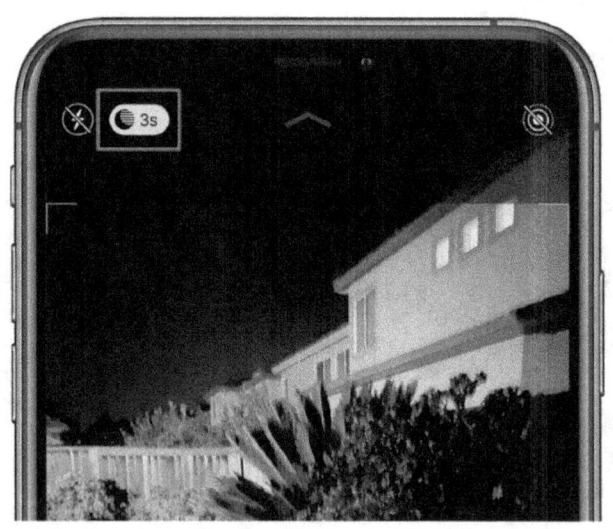

Figure 49: Night Mode Feature Activated

The yellow icon displays the number of seconds (like 1 second, 3 seconds) it will take for the camera to capture the scene from start to finish. The number of seconds displayed is used to determine how long the shutter button has to be pressed down to capture the night shot. This time also can be adjusted. Set too high, and you run the risk of your photo suffering from overexposure, whereas setting it too low will result in a dark photo.

You do have an option to disable the Night mode also by tapping on the Night Mode icon sliding the slider next to the shutter button. For scenes not brightly lit, the Night mode option then becomes available even though it is not yet enabled. You can tell it is not activated if the yellow icon is not highlighted. In such situations, you have to manually tap it to enable it if you think the photo will benefit from the Night mode feature, once switched on, the white Night mode icon turns to yellow.

Night mode adds more details to the final image after brightening the shots in such poor illuminated situations

The Night Mode requires some form of light from a lamp, bulb, or street light to be in the scene where the photo is going to be taken. The exposure time can be set to Auto or adjusted with the slider at the bottom. To increase or decrease the exposure time, simply drag the slider accordingly.

When the shutter button is pressed to take a shot, the yellow slider starts counting down the timer to the end of the exposure, you only have to ensure you're either shooting with the 1x Wide lens or the 2x Telephoto lens for the Night mode to work since the Night Mode doesn't work with the 0.5x Ultra-Wide lens. The iPhone 11 Pro's Night mode is one of the most important camera settings on the iPhone 11 and iPhone 11 Pro.

- Tap Camera on the phone to launch it up
- The Camera app can automatically identify poorly lit conditions and change it into night mode. You can also manually turn on the night mode by tapping the night mode button
- A slider that displays the auto recommended time would appear under the frame. Use the slider to increase or decrease the exposure time manually

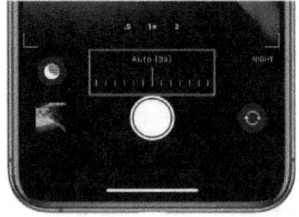

Figure 50: Setting Exposure Duration for Capturing Night Mode Images

- Tap the shutter button to initiate the shooting process
- Hold the camera very still while the timer counts down to zero as it takes a series of pictures that it combines to produce the final output

For best output when you want to take a picture in Night mode with long exposure time for as long as 30 seconds, you are better off with a tripod. The gyroscope works in such situations by detecting if the phone is absolutely still so that it can count down on the long exposure time.

Taking a Live Photo

A Live Photo is used to capture what happened just before and what happens just after you take your photo. It is a feature that allows you to shoot a 3-second moving image recording with the surrounding audio.

A Live Photo will capture 1.5 seconds before, and 1.5 seconds after the shutter is pressed, it is, therefore, important to ensure the camera stays still a few moments before and after the shutter button is tapped.

It's usually ideal for those situations where a video may be an overkill, and a still image isn't sufficient. It is very useful in bringing an image to life with just a few seconds of motion and sound.

Before shooting a Live Photo, it is important to always ensure the Live Photo icon at the top right of the screen is switched on.

To take advantage of the live photo, follow the steps below.

- Tap the camera app to launch it
- Tap the Live Photos button to turn it off or on
- Tap the Shutter button to take the shot now

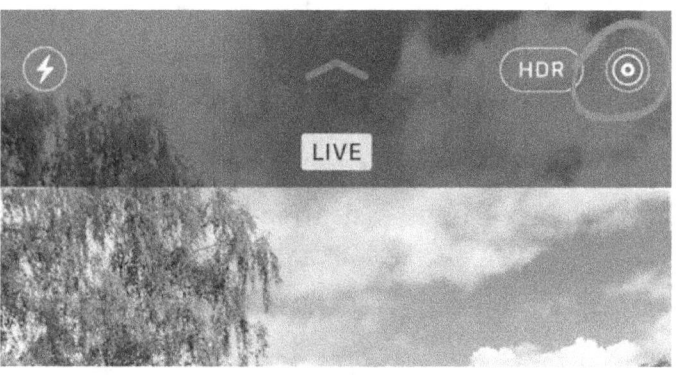

Figure 51: Live Photo Button

Viewing a Live Photo

After taking a live photo, you may want to view the photo to see the result of your action, the best way to achieve that is to view the Live Photo.

To view the Live Photo

- Tap the Photos app to open it

- Tap the image from the gallery of what you want to open
- Hold your finger on the image to play the Live Photo.

Viewing Custom Effects of a Live Photo

To see other effects on the Live Photo, you can swipe up on the opened Live Photo, and four other Effects will be displayed.

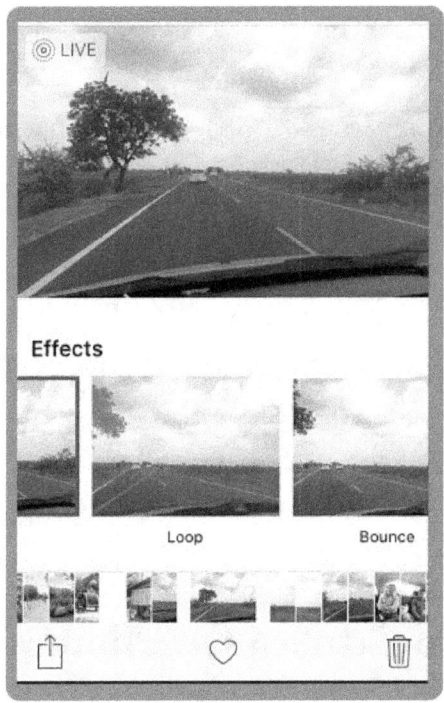

Figure 52: Creating Effects with Live Photo

You can see all the other hidden ones by scrolling across the effects.

Types of Live Photo Effects

Live

This is the default Live Photo that is used to play a 3-second Life Photo video clip

Loop

Loop will play a continuous Live video loop Photo

Bounce

Bounce will play a Live Photo in the forward direction and then play the reverse direction. This it does continuously

Long Exposure

This can be used to create a still photo with a slow shutter effect. It is also able to blur any movement in the scene, which makes it a very simple way of creating amazing pictures of a long exposure like rivers or swimming pools.

To Edit a Live Photos

- Tap the Photos app to open it
- You can identify live photos with the inscription 'Live" somewhere around the corner

- Go ahead to edit the Live Photos

Taking a Panorama Photo

The Pano mode is useful when capturing landscapes or other shots that cannot easily fit into your camera screen. To use the Pano mode, follow the steps below.

- Tap to open the Camera app
- Select the Pano mode
- Tap the Shutter button
- Pan gradually in the direction of the arrow and ensure it is on the centerline
- Tap the shutter button again to round up the process
- To pan in the other direction, use the arrow
- To pan vertically, you can rotate the iPhone to a landscape orientation
- To pan horizontally, you can rotate the iPhone to a Portrait orientation

Taking a Photo with a Filter

You are also able to take pictures by adding filters at the point of taking the pictures by following these steps.

- Open the Camera app
- Choose Photo or Portrait mode
- Tap the arrow pointing up

- Tap the filter button

- Under the viewer, swipe the filters around from left to right to preview the effects

- Tap on any of them to select it

Any filter added when taking the picture can be changed or removed with the Photos app

Recording a Slow-motion Video

Slo-mo videos record the same way regular videos do, and they exhibit the slo-mo effects when they are played back. The videos can also be edited so that the slo-mo actions can be made to start or stop at any time you want.

- Open the Camera app

- Select the Slo-mo mode from the options

- Tap the Record button or use the volume button to also start and stop the recording

- You can still snap a still photo while the recording is going on by pressing the shutter button

- You can also set a part of the video to play in slow motion while other parts can play at regular speed by tapping the video thumbnail of the particular video

- Then tap Edit and slide the vertical bars under the frame viewer when defining the section, you want the slow-motion playback to happen

75

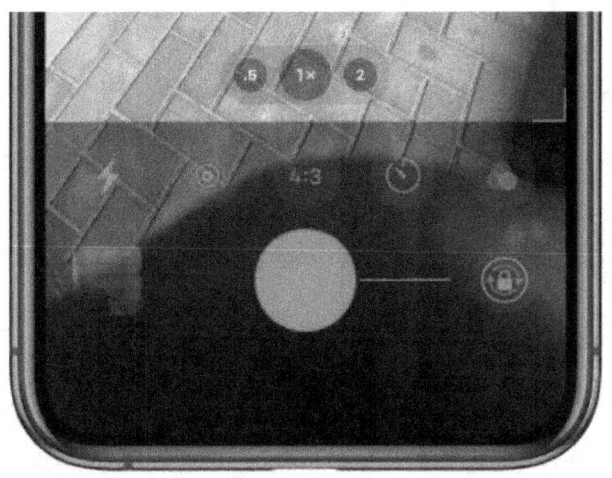

Figure 53: Slo-Mo Capture of Images

Adjusting the Camera Focus

The general rule with taking pictures with the iPhone 11 Pro as well as with other devices is to hold the shutter or tap the subject you want to focus on as you await a white box appearing enclosing the subject. Still holding the screen, you wait for the white square to turn yellow, indicating the camera has locked its focus, after which you can then take the picture.

It can sometimes take a while to be able to focus on the subject finally, but the quality of the pictures will more than compensate for the effort.

Manually Adjusting the Camera Focus

The iPhone 11 Pro can automatically adjust its camera's focus when you are trying to take a picture to produce sharp-focused images. However, there are those who want to exercise more control over what part of the scene they want to be in focus rather than relying on what the camera decides to be the area of focus.

To manually set the focus of your camera on a section of a scene, you simply tap the screen where you want to set your focus, as you await a white box appearing enclosing the subject. Still holding the screen, you wait for the white square to turn yellow, indicating the camera has locked its focus, after which you can then take the picture by tapping the shutter button.

If the photos you want to take with the focus set at the same point are many, you can opt to have the focus locked. To do that, you have to tap and hold the screen on where you want the focus to be set until you see the AE/AF lock showing at the top of the screen, after which you release your finger.

With focus locked, as many photos as you want can then be taken without the need to change the focus point. Whenever you want to deactivate the locked focus, simply tap anywhere on the screen, and the AE/AF will become disabled.

Manually setting the camera focus allows users to have more control over what parts of an image can appear clear and sharp over the others. When used correctly, this is one simple iPhone camera trick that can turn you into an iPhone photography professional.

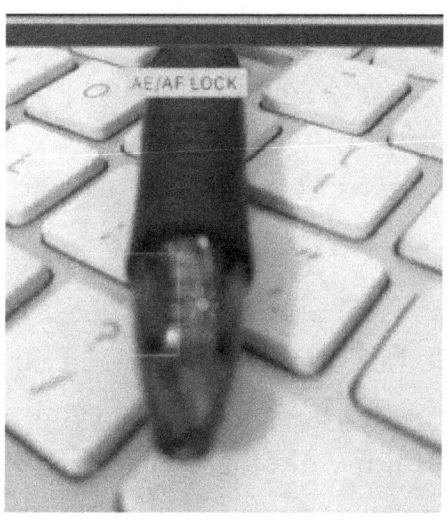

Figure 54: Locking Camera Focus

How to Adjust the Camera Exposure

One other fantastic feature the iPhone 11 Pro camera comes with is the ability of the camera to fix photos that appear too dark or too bright. When you have a balanced exposure that does not have any very bright or dark areas that can make the image too bright or too dark, the image can retain its details and color.

To use this feature on the iPhone, you have to attempt to focus on the subject, as explained in the explanation on focusing. When the white square appears on the screen, you will notice a sun icon beside the white line. As soon as the white square changes to a yellow line, you can then move your finger up and down the slider to change the exposure level to what you want by monitoring how bright or dark the image on the screen is in real-time.

For situations where you want the photo to be a silhouette photo for it to have a dark or completely black appearance, the exposure level will need to be reduced more than normal.

Imagine you want to create an image of a sunset photo, using this simple but powerful slider you take control of the exposure of your photo and significantly improve the quality of your iPhone photography. This is one iPhone 11 Pro feature not many people either know how to use or that it exists at all.

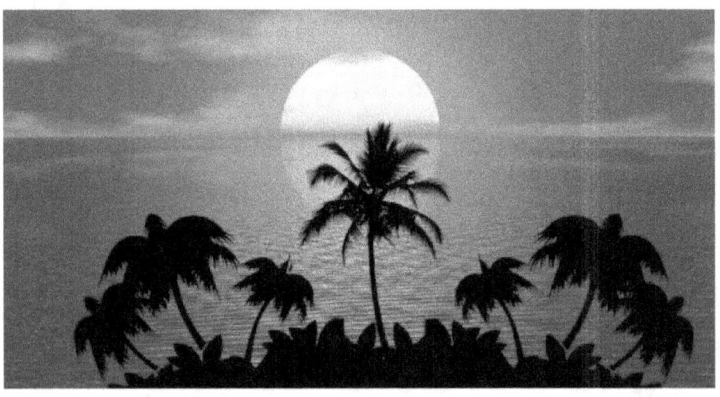

Figure 55: Adjusting Exposure for Effect

How to Adjust the Filter of the iPhone

To use the filter feature of the iPhone 11 Pro, first;

- Launch the Camera app

- Tap on the filter button 🔘 with three overlapping circle icon at the screen's top right corner

- Choose from any of the available selections and begin taking your pictures

If, after taking the image with a predefined filter and you later do not like what you see, you can then use the Photo app on the iPhone to alter the preset of filter you applied to your image at any time without significantly affecting the quality of the picture.

The photo app on the iPhone does not, in this case, overlay the filter over the already existing one, instead, it replaces it so that you do not have a photograph with oversaturated unnatural colors.

How to Use the Self-Timer

Tap the timer icon on the iPhone 11 Pro screen. By tapping it, you can choose either the 3-second or the 10-second timer options.

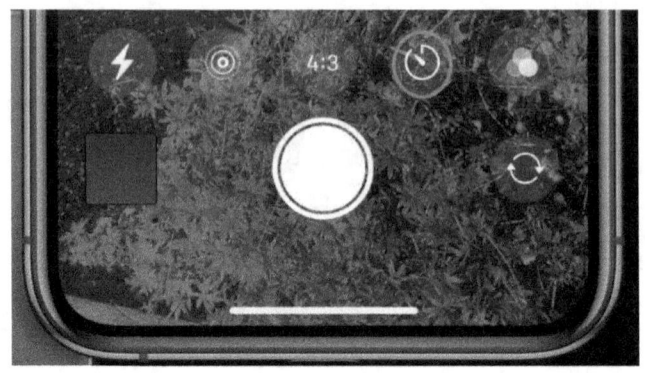

Figure 56: Setting the Camera Self-timer

The timer option works best when used with a suitable tripod stand so that you can set your camera in position without worrying about the camera moving out of focus or out of position when the picture is being taken.

Creating Fun Stuff

The new iPhone 11 Pro allows users to create multiple personalized Memojis that can be used to show their different moods by selecting skin color, hairstyle, facial expressions, earrings, glasses, and other personalized imitations.

This feature is possible by the presence of the iPhone 11 Pro TrueDepth camera's features which makes it possible to analyze over 50 muscle movements of a person's face by detecting and recording the movement in a person's eye and eyebrow, lips, mouth, jaw, cheeks, and chin. These facial features are then transmitted to the Animoji and Memoji characters such that they can express emotions similar to the way you would display those kinds of emotions and expressions. The Animoji and Memojis can then be shared with others in the form of messages and FaceTime apps.

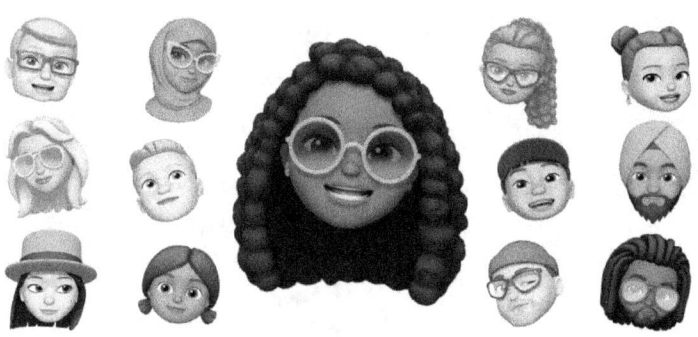

Figure 57: Have Fun with your iPhone 11 Pro

Apple has these Animojis modeled as emoji characters like robots, cat, dog, alien, chicken, dragon, ghost, fox, and many other emoji characters that a user can choose from.

With iPhone 11 Pro's Animoji and Memoji stickers, users can create records of their voices alongside the mirroring of their facial expressions in ways that create stickers that match their personalities and moods effectively.

How to Create your Own Memoji

- When in a conversation, tap the plus sign

- Tap the Memoji symbol 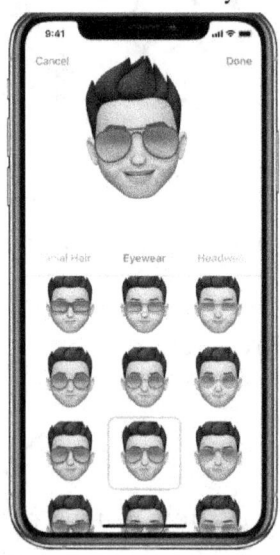, swipe right and tap New Memoji

- Browse through the various Memojis and select the character you like.

- Bring your character to life by adding personalized features that fit your personality to the Memoji.

- When you get satisfied with the outcome, tap Done to add the Memoji to your collection for future use or Cancel to discard your changes

Figure 58: Time to Create Me from my Memoji

To Edit, Duplicate, or Delete a Memoji

If you are no longer interested in retaining a Memoji, you can either make changes to create a more appropriate image of what you want, or you can delete it if the need arises. Follow the steps below to do that.

- Tap the Memoji app and select the three dots at the top right corner
- Select Edit to make the changes or select delete to remove the Memoji from the collections
- Select Done when through or Cancel to discard changes

Sending Animated Animoji or Memoji Recordings

For Animoji and Memoji messages that make use of your voice alongside the mirroring of the expressions on your face, you can create it and send it using the following steps.

- When in a conversation in messenger or tap the button to start a message ✏️
- Tap the feature button 🐵 to select Animoji or Memoji, swipe left and pick a character
- Tap the record button to start the recording of your voice and facial expression
- To stop recording, tap the red square
- To view your message, select and tap the Replay button

- If satisfied with the outcome, tap the arrow button to send the message or select the delete button to discard the message

Another thing you can do is take a picture or video of yourself as an Animoji or Memoji and add stickers to it before sending, which you can then use in a FaceTime conversation if you prefer to hide your true identity or want to have some fun.

Third-party Camera Apps

When it comes to photography, the Camera app on the iPhone 11 Pro does such a great job. Capturing images is as easy as the press of a button, however, if you are looking to take advantage of the kind of Cameras on the iPhone, then you may need to consider a few third-party Camera apps.

Camera+ 2

A popular Camera app for the iPhone has to be Camera+2. It has a feel of the native camera app, yet it offers a whole new world of photographic features. It offers extra features like the ability to take Raw shots, gridlines alongside basic functions like continuous flash, 6x digital zoom, and timer. It even has a mode that attempts to detect smiles on persons and a slow shutter when taking long exposures.

Obscura 2

Obscura 2 is best known for its clean and simple interface, unlike other camera apps that bog users down with functions that may be confusing. This app was built to be minimal while helping you to take much better photos. It has a few controls to work with via dials on the screen to control more than 19 inbuilt filters that you can use when taking pictures and even proceed to edit your photographs further and make your work easier.

Many photographers consider it a useful app to have on their iPhone, especially those hoping to take the leap into more professional features. The camera app also has support for RAW captures alongside JPEG, Live Photo, and Apple's default HEIC format. There are even options for depth capture mode, grid overlay, flash control and manual controls for various tweaks you may want to make

VSCO

This Camera app can also pass as a photo editing app and a very good one at that. With VSCO, you can shoot RAW images and manually control features like exposure, brightness, and lots more. It has a user-friendly interface for both editing and capturing images.

Beyond the simple manual controls, there are many other advanced features, many of which may require a pro-level subscription to unlock. The VSCO also stands out in the area of filters, where you can pick a preset to start editing the images.

Halide

With Halide, you can manually control the photography process. You can use it to set everything from exposure to focus to shutter speed to ISO and lots more.

Although it has an interface that can be intimidating at first glance, it, however, has views for histograms, depth peaking, monitoring of the phone registering, and depth of field settings. If any of these terms sound strange to you, then nothing to worry about as Halide is probably not a feature you want to bother about since it is primarily designed for professional photographers who wish to have better control of the image capturing process rather than having to leave things to automatic settings alone. It is considered by many iPhone users to be one of the best camera apps for iOS devices.

ProCamera

If you shoot a considerable number of videos, then ProCamera should be an app of choice for you. Although very similar to other Camera apps, it provides in-depth control that you can use to manipulate and edit things like the HDR, low light, frame rate, and resolution of your videos.

It doesn't stop there, it also includes some advanced settings for controlling features like geotagging, stabilization, file format, and focusing.

Chapter 6

CRCRCR

Configuring Other Camera Settings

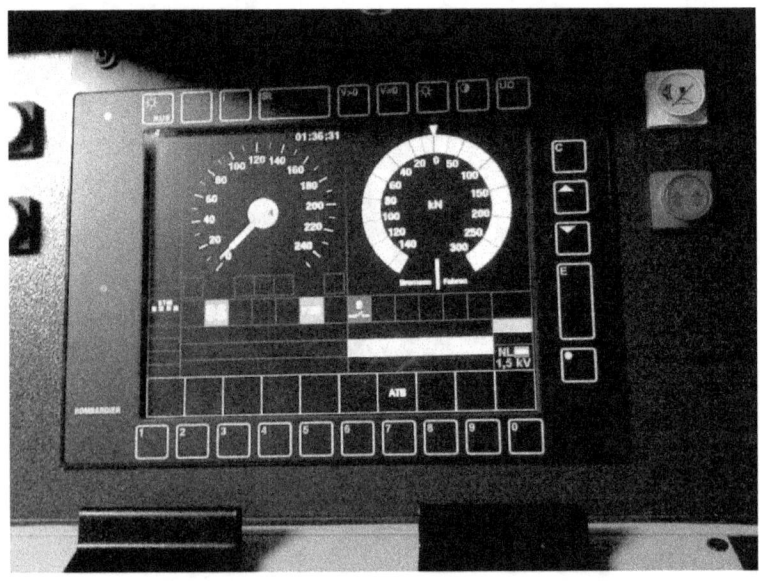

As you may have noticed from what we've covered so far, the iPhone camera seems really simple to manipulate, however, as you will soon find out, there are a few other things that on the surface look easy but do require some level of more in-depth knowledge.

Even though the iPhone 11 Pro comes with standard functions that are easy to navigate, there are several other important camera settings that are usually not immediately obvious except you are able to find your way around the phone.

To access many of these other functions, tap on the arrow at the top of the phone's screen with the iPhone in a vertical position or on the left when the phone is in a horizontal position. This will reveal the various hidden toggles, which can then be hidden again when you tap the button again as soon as you're done. Another way to show the toggles is to swipe across the viewfinder.

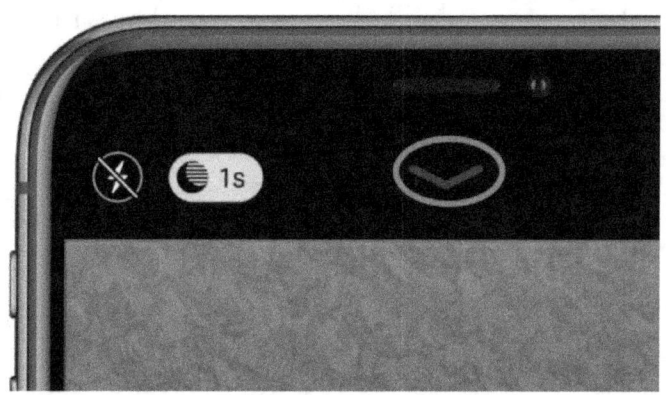

Figure 59: Opening More iPhone 11 Pro Camera Features

Accessing Hidden Camera Controls

When you tap the up arrow at the top of the iPhone 11 Pro screen or just swipe up on the viewfinder to access more controls, a row of icons just above the shutter button will appear.

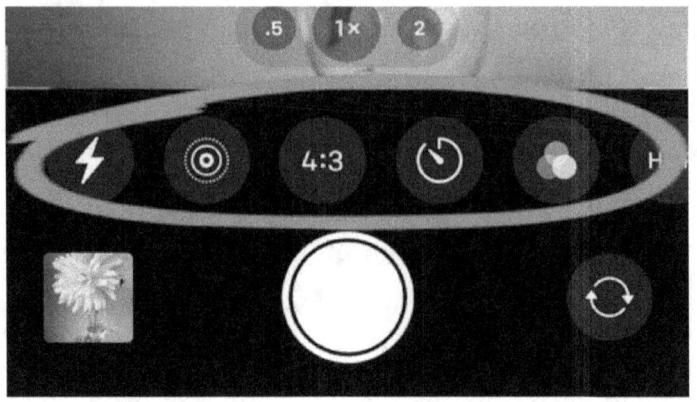

Figure 60: Using Advanced Camera Controls

Some of the icons you will already be familiar with, others may seem confusing for now. To describe them from left to right, we have:

- Flash
- Night mode
- Live Photos
- Aspect Ratio
- Timer
- Filters
- HDR

This option provides an alternative of accessing the Night mode, Live Photos, and HDR since we already know that they can easily be accessed from the icons at the top of the screen. It's usually better to keep the Flash setting switched off, except you feel there is a need to add to the illumination of the scene with extra light from the flash. You can, however, tap any of the flash buttons to set it on, off, or put it on auto.

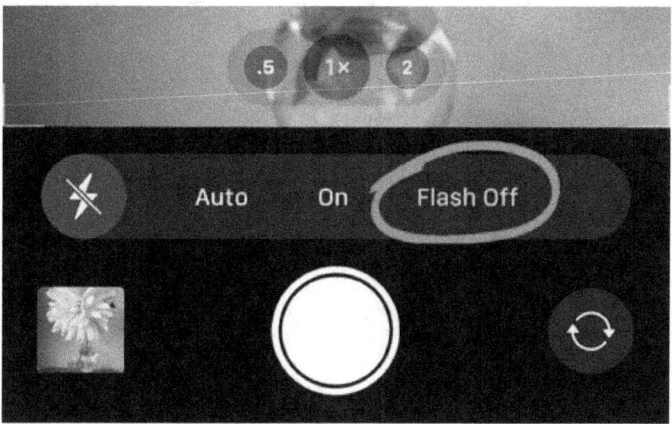

Figure 61: Setting the iPhone 11 Pro Flash

Images on the iPhone 11 Pro can be captured in any one of three aspect ratios that include Square, 4:3 ratio (which uses the standard rectangle), or the 16:9 ratio (which uses the wide specification).

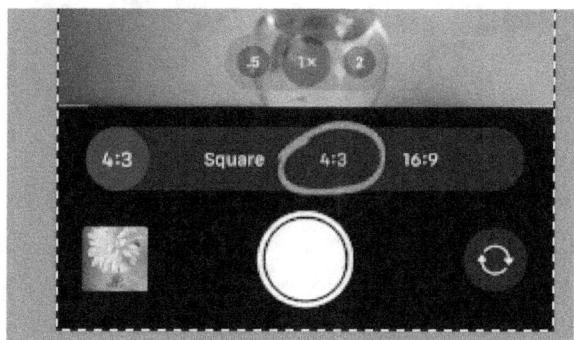

Figure 62: Manipulating Aspect Ratio

The Square and 16:9 ratios tend to always crop out parts of images when a photo is being shot, which is why it is usually better to have photos shot in the full 4:3 aspect ratio. That way, if you feel the need to crop the image to a different aspect ratio, you can easily do that using the iPhone 11 Pro's Photos app or any other photo editing app.

The timer icon can be used to set a delay time of 3 seconds or 10 seconds between when the shutter is pressed, and when the photo is captured.

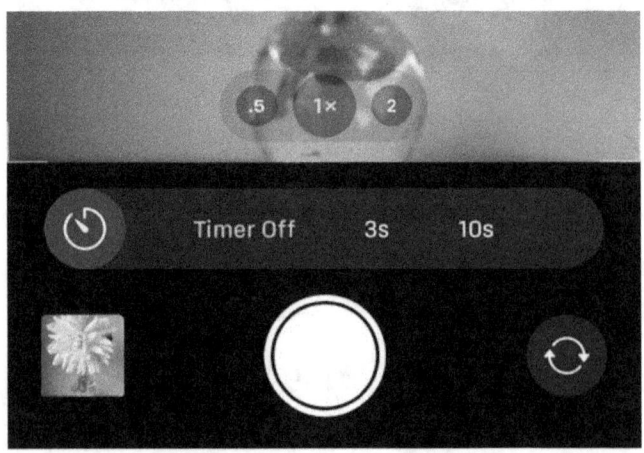

Figure 63: Setting Camera Timer

The iPhone camera timer is handy when you want to shoot a picture of yourself or group shots that you want to be in. A tripod can also be used for the photos to ensure the camera stays steady, especially for photos that require long exposures.

The Filters icon grants you access to a wide range of preset filters you can use to change various outlooks of your image.

Depending on the filter selected, some of them have warm colors, others have cool colors while others have black and white filters. Any of these filters can produce a unique effect on the images or photos they are applied to.

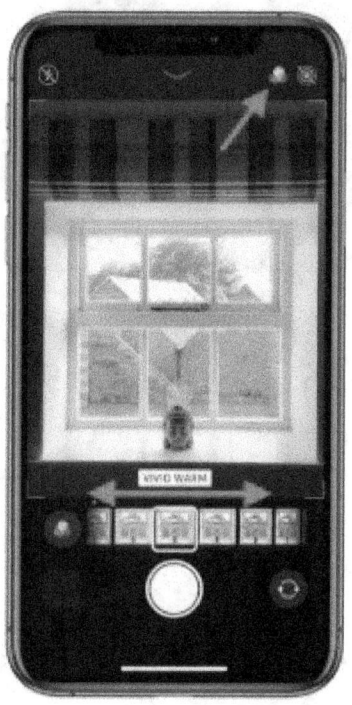

Figure 64: Applying Filters

Photos can also have these filters applied or removed from them when pictures are edited in the Photos app. A lot of people find that it is simpler to capture a scene with no filter and have the filter applied later when processing the image.

When taking pictures without applying filters, it is important to ensure that the filter is selected is the Original.

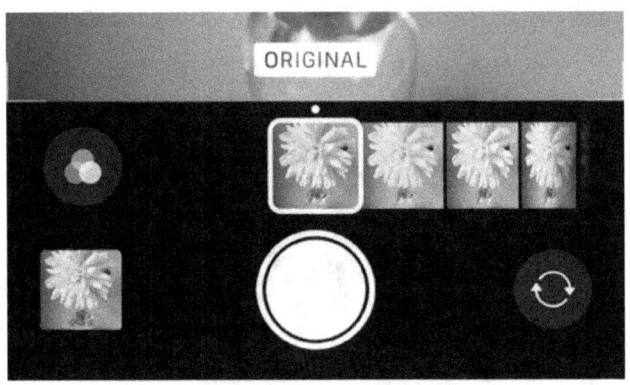

Figure 65: Using the Default Filter

Once you are done using these hidden features, you can decide to hide them again with the controls of the camera at the bottom of the screen. You can then swipe down on the viewfinder or tap the down arrow at the top of the screen.

Using the HDR Feature

A lot of people find shooting scenes with high-contrast to be tricky. Many digital cameras, especially phone cameras, struggle to capture details in areas that are very dark and bright at the same time. But not so with the Smart HDR feature that the iPhone 11 Pro Camera app comes with.

HDR enables users to capture incredible details of scenes in both the shadow and the highlights.

Just like the Night Mode feature, the HDR works by taking multiple shots of a scene by using different exposures whenever the shutter is pressed. To create the final output, the advanced iPhone software merges the images to create a single, clear, and crisp image with great color and corresponding details.

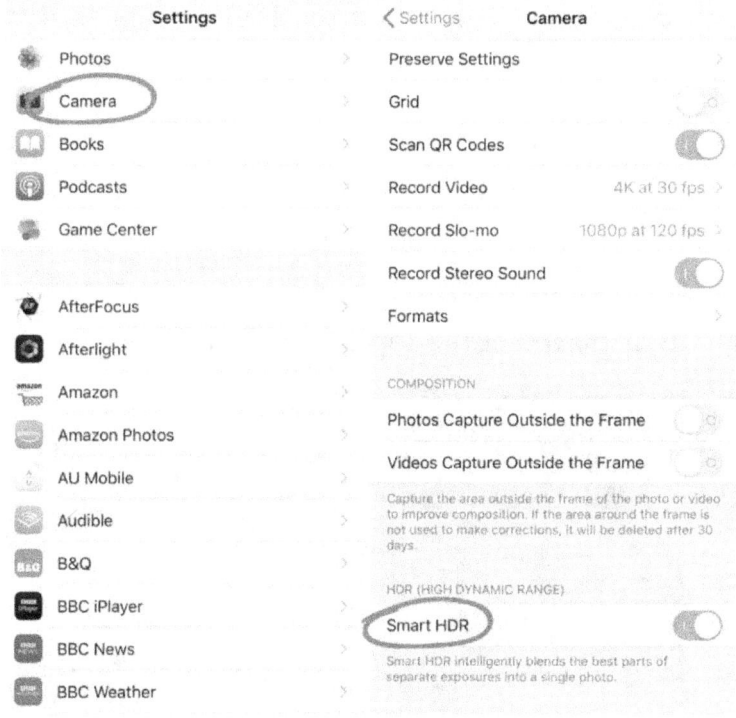

Figure 66: Activating Smart HDR on the iPhone 11 Pro

To take an HDR photo on iPhone 11 Pro, you have to first enable the feature in the iPhone 11 Pro Settings app.

- Open the Settings app
- Select Camera
- Toggle the Smart HDR option towards the bottom of the screen

It is always good practice to keep the Smart HDR on. With the Smart HDR switched on, the iPhone is now able to shoot HDR photos automatically whenever the need arises, so you do not have to bother yourself about whether or not you need to use the HDR when shooting a scene.

However, you still have the option to decide to switch off the Smart HDR if you want to be able to exercise better control over when the Smart HDR kicks in or not. To know if your Smart HDR is switched on, you will see the HDR icon displayed at the top of the Camera app.

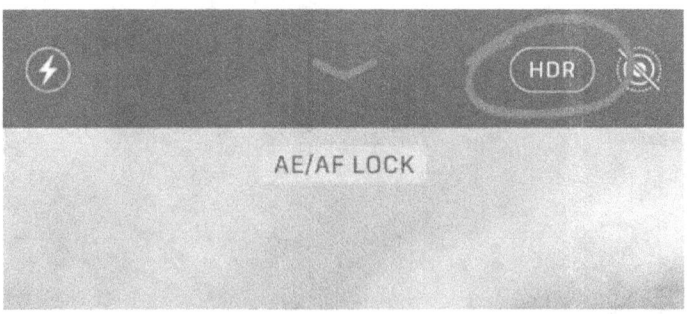

Figure 67: Smart HDR On

The HDR icon can also be used to toggle the HDR On and Off, which can easily be differentiated with a line across the icon, indicating that the HDR is switched off.

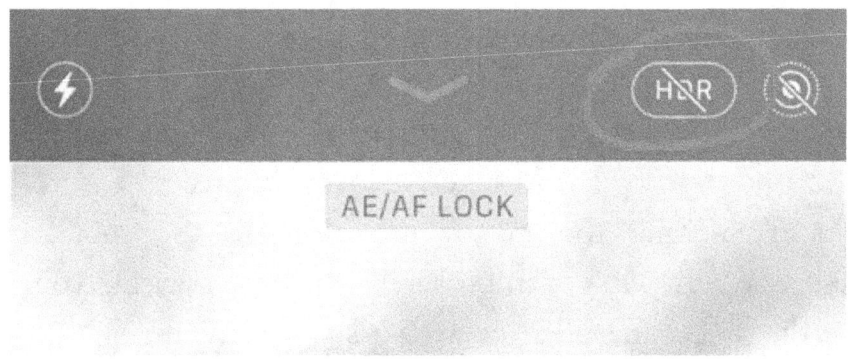

Figure 68: Smart HDR Off

Images shot with the HDR activated on the iPhone 11 Pro tend to have very good color and detail in the shadows as well as the highlights. Without the Smart HDR switched on, some sections of a photo can be too bright compared to if the Smart HDR was on. With the Smart HDR on, many problems associated with exposure encountered when shooting high contrasting scenes can be avoided.

Blurring Photos Backgrounds with Portrait Mode

If you have ever wondered how people take pictures of a subject while blurring other aspects of the photos, then you have the portrait mode to thank for that. With portrait mode, your picture can focus on you alone and remove other parts of the pictures that may want to serve as a source of distraction.

To use the Portrait mode in the iPhone 11 Pro Camera app, you tap the portrait mode to the left of the Photo mode below the viewfinder and above the shutter. A frame will be displayed on the screen around the subject who photo you want to take a shot, you have to ensure you are neither too far or too close to the subject otherwise you will get an on-screen message advising you to adjust your distance from the subject. When on the Portrait mode, you also have the option to switch between the 2x Telephoto or the 1x Wide lens simply by tapping 1x or 2x at the bottom left corner of the screen.

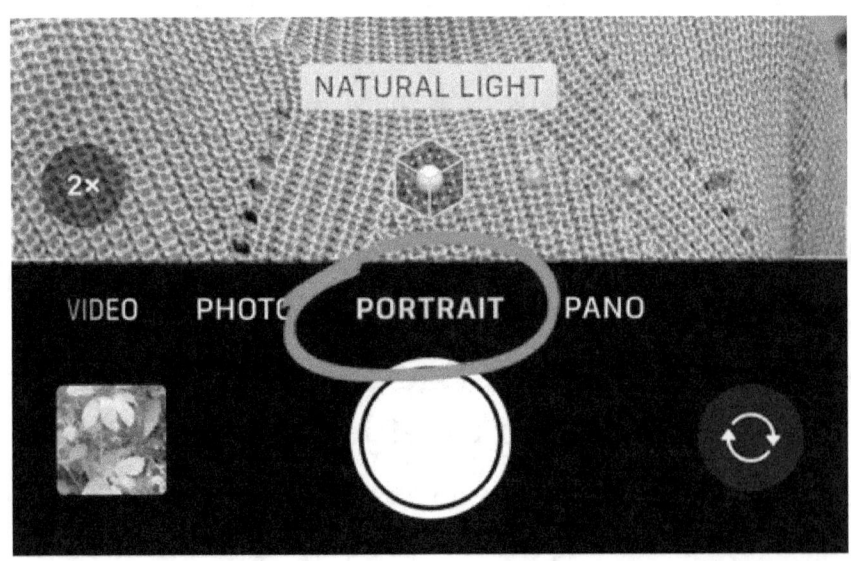

Figure 69: Portrait Mode on iPhone 11 Pro

Portrait mode is an amazing feature to use in shooting amazing portraits of people's photos, which helps to keep the person in sharp focus while blurring the background. Interestingly, portrait mode also works well for many other foreground objects, flowers, and pets.

To know that the Portrait mode is active, the words Natural Light appears in yellow on the screen, at that point, you can now tap the shutter button to take your shot.

With the picture taken in portrait mode, you are now able to adjust the strength of the blurring of the background and also use Portrait Lighting to apply some effects like studio light to your image even though many of these settings are better off adjusting after taking the photo.

Adjusting Portrait Photos

To modify your images on the iPhone 11 Pro including Portrait photos, you use the Photos app on the iPhone

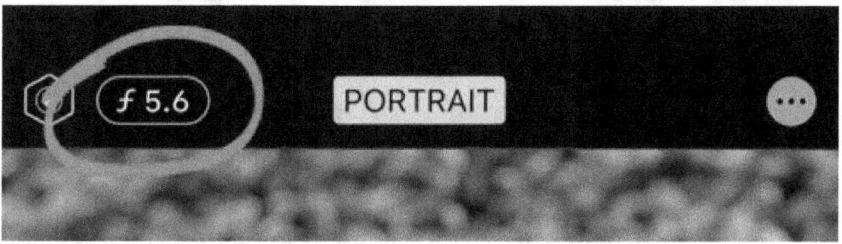

Figure 70: Adjusting the F-Number

- Tap the image to open it in the Photos app

100

- Tap Edit.
- Tap the f-number icon at the top left corner of the screen to have the strength of the background blur adjusted

To adjust the strength of the background blur, you drag the Depth slider at the lower part of the screen to adjust the f-number. A smaller f-number will make the background of the scene more blurred, whereas a high f-number will make it seem less blurred.

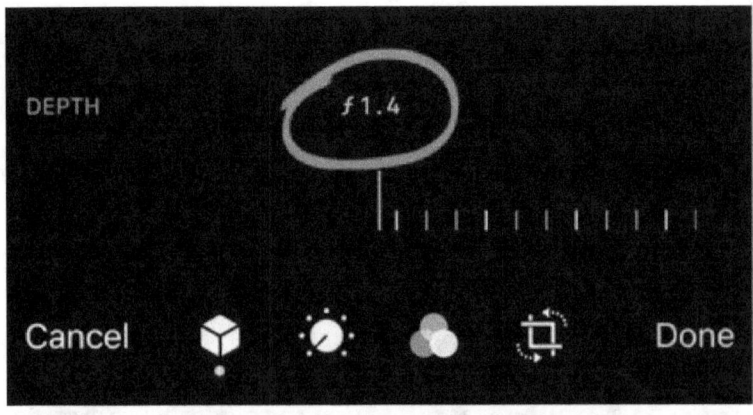

Figure 71: Setting the F-Number

If you want the lighting effect to be adjusted, you'd have to tap the Portrait Lighting icon, which has the shape of a hexagon at the top left and the icons for Portrait Lighting will appear below the photo.

You can then scroll through the different effects to select the one you want from the various options that include, but not limited to Studio Light, Contour Light, and Stage Light.

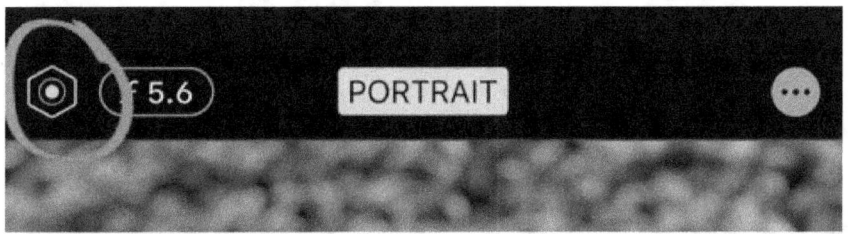

Figure 72: Controlling the Portrait Lighting Icon

Once an option has been selected, the slider below the screen can then be used to adjust how intense the light effect should be.

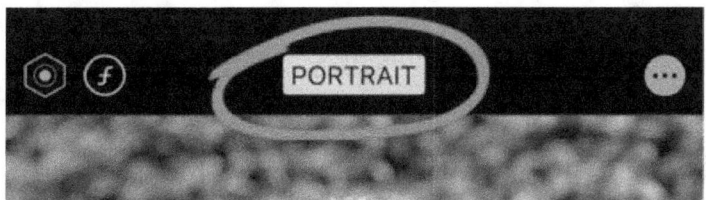

Figure 73: Portrait Mode Active

The best way to see the effect of each of them is to play around with them.

How Not to Include the Blur

If you decide against having the background of your photo blurred, you have the option to remove the blur effect.

To remove the blur;

- Tap Portrait at the top of the screen to deactivate the Portrait mode
- To switch the blur back on, tap Portrait again
- Tap Done to save the changes or Cancel to discard the changes

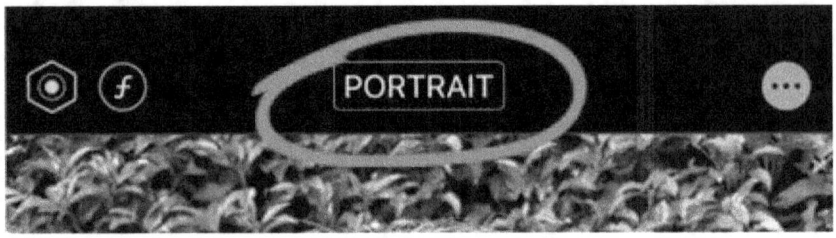

Figure 74: Portrait Mode Inactive

You can then view the output of your Portrait shot as soon as you complete the required adjustments to your Portrait mode photo.

Conclusion

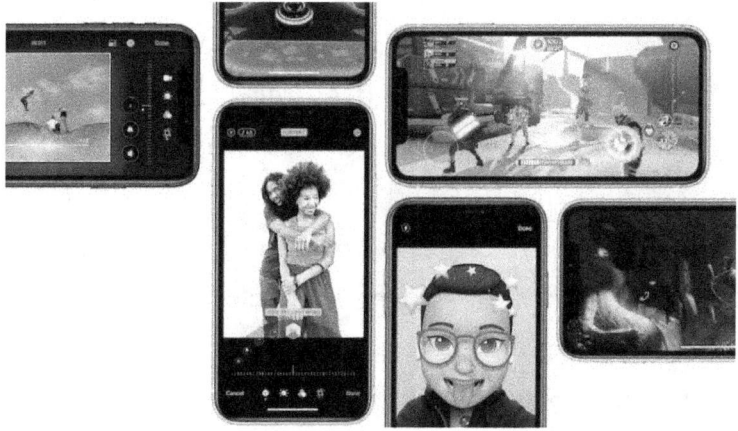

The iPhone 11 Pro has many new photo and video features designed to improve the photo shooting experience of iPhone users and social media fanatics. It has provisions for both beginners, advanced photographers, and videographers. For the first time, Apple responded to the request by users for a Night mode feature optimized for low-light settings.

The automatic setting on the iPhone 11 Pro is now very good at adjusting settings like focus, exposure, shutter speed, and ISO in the capturing of sharp, bright and crisp images. The portrait mode on the iPhone 11 Pro wide-angle lens can be used to work with pets, and you can easily swap from just taking pictures into making a video very easily using the QuickTake feature in the same way the burst function on previous iPhone used to be done. That means the burst mode is achieved differently from how it used to be.

The iPhone 11 Pro camera has been described as one of the best cameras to have ever been released by Apple and rightly so, and it is not hard to see why. Apple added many features that make the Camera a significant improvement from earlier versions. For starters, the iPhone 11 Pro now has three rear cameras, a standard wide-angle one, a wide-lens one and a telephoto lens on the physical level and a Night mode at the software level.

This book was written to introduce you to some of those features that this fantastic phone offers and ensure you have a good user experience when using the camera feature of the iPhone 11 Pro. With this book, you can immediately get started by exploring the amazing photo feature of this iPhone.